This book is about the quest
for a satisfying spirituality.

This book was read by

_____

_____

DATE

This book was a gift from

_____

WHO SHOULD READ THIS BOOK

This book is for anyone—Jew and non-Jew, Jew-by-Choice and Jew-by-Birth—who seeks to understand why converts choose Judaism, how the process of conversion unfolds, and how Judaism can quench a spiritual thirst. In particular, it is for:

- Those who have already converted as well as those who are considering conversion. They will find a voice here which they understand and which speaks to them and for them.

- Immediate family members of a Jew-by-Choice—the non-Jewish family which provided his or her spiritual beginnings and the Jewish family which receives the convert. They will gain insight into the decision to convert.

- Jews-by-Birth, who can newly appreciate Judaism's beauties and traditions by viewing Judaism through the eyes of the convert.

- Rabbis and Jewish educators who work with converts, to help them further appreciate their students' sincerity, commitment and spiritual diversity.

- The Jewish community, to help deepen its understanding of the journeys taken by converts.

HOW TO USE THIS BOOK

Embracing the Covenant reflects the deep feelings, attitudes and commitments of many converts to Judaism. Because their stories are grouped in four sections, each with its own theme, this book can be read cover to cover or can be read one section at a time.

If you are exploring your own relationship with God, the essays in Section I, "The Search for God and Spirituality," will guide your process. If Judaism's strengths interest you, Section II, "The Appeals of Judaism," will intrigue you. If you are on a spiritual journey, Section III, "Journeys to Judaism," will introduce you to "fellow travelers." And if you are exploring ways to express your faith, Section IV, "Turning Faith into Action," will inspire you.

By reading this book cover to cover, you will understand the conversion process, Judaism's multitude of attractions, and the many types of Jews-by-Choice and what brings them to Judaism.

By reading this book in sections, you will gain understanding into particular aspects of Judaism, conversion, and the lives of converts.

Each section of the book includes pages of "Gleanings": brief quotes from Jews-by-Choice that focus on a single issue. We hope that they will provoke thoughts and questions, as well as offer additional insights for you, the reader.

EMBRACING
THE
COVENANT

Converts to Judaism

Talk About Why & How

EDITED AND WITH INTRODUCTIONS BY

Rabbi Allan L. Berkowitz

&

Patti Moskovitz

JEWISH LIGHTS PUBLISHING

Woodstock, Vermont

Embracing the Covenant:
Converts to Judaism Talk about Why & How

2005 Fourth Printing
2001 Third Printing
1998 Second Printing
1996 First Printing

Library of Congress Cataloging-in-Publication Data
Embracing the covenant : converts to Judaism talk about why & how / edited by Allan Berkowitz & Patti Moskovitz.
p.   cm.
Includes bibliographical references.
ISBN 1-879045-50-8 (pbk.)
1. Proselytes and proselyting, Jewish—Converts from Christianity—biography.   2. Jews—United States—Biography.   I. Berkowitz, Allan, 1957–.
II. Moskovitz, Patti, 1940–.
BM729.P7E57   1996
296.714—dc20   96-5159
                                                                    CIP

10   9   8   7   6   5   4

Manufactured in the United States of America
Book and cover designed by Karen Savary
Cover art: "My Kindness Shall not depart from you,
          Neither shall my covenant of peace be removed"
                                                    (Isaiah 54:10)
Linen fiber sculpture 40 x 60 x 3"
Artist: Laurie Gross, © 1986
Photo: Marvin Rand

Published by Jewish Lights Publishing
A Division of LongHill Partners, Inc.
Sunset Farm Offices, Route 4, P.O. Box 237
Woodstock, VT   05091
Tel: (802) 457-4000   Fax: (802) 457-4004
www.jewishlights.com

For my students—Jewish stars who shine bright.
For "The Brady Bunch"—
Rebecca, Elisha, Abigail and Eitan.
And especially for Mindy—this book (and my heart)
could not have been completed without you.
—ALLAN BERKOWITZ

To Larry, my wonderful husband and heart's dearest
companion. And to my children, the lights of my life.
To my students, who inspired this book and
illuminate my Jewish path.
And to my beloved parents of blessed memory,
Vera and David Kipnis and Beatrice and Albert Moskovitz,
my true teachers.
—PATTI MOSKOVITZ

CONTENTS

INTRODUCTION

THIS BOOK HAD ITS INCEPTION SEVEN YEARS AGO.
In fact, in Judaism the number "seven" is significant: It symbolizes
completeness, rest and holiness. Just as God rested on the seventh
day, Jews also rest to restore their souls. During Judaism's morning prayers, the *tefillin* (phylacteries containing the words of the
Jewish commandments) are wrapped around the arm seven times
to remind us of six days of creation followed by a seventh day of
rest. In the Jewish wedding ceremony, the bride circles the groom
seven times. Just as a wedding is a sacred embrace, a conversion is,
also, since it offers the soul rest and completeness after a long spiritual journey.

The Jewish people are a nation of converts and born-Jews,
of people born into the Jewish faith and of people who have
come from other faiths. This latter category included Abraham,
the first patriarch of the Jews, who journeyed to a new and
strange land at the behest of a compelling, demanding Voice.
Throughout millennia, those who have become Jews have

responded to the beckoning of that same Voice, leaving the familiar behind them as they find a new spiritual family and a home.

The life-stories in this book may be seen as love-stories. They chronicle the course of lives forever changed by a murmuring in the soul and a reverberating in the heart. Just as humans fall in love, utterly beyond reason and logic, so, too, does the Jew-by-Choice cleave to God and to the Jewish people. This embrace touches and forever changes both the Jew-by-Birth and the Jew-by-Choice.

Just what is it that the Jew-by-Choice embraces? The question seems simple; the answer is fascinating in its complexity. Judaism is often seen as a "religion," a "culture," a "civilization" or a "way of life." To contemplate what Judaism is is to enter a room which has many doors, all leading to the same chamber. Each of us has available to us these different ways to enter that room. Similarly, one may find and express one's Jewish heritage through Jewish history. Or through rituals and observances. Or through the culture or "ethos" of the Jewish People. Or through the Hebrew language. If the chamber cannot be entered through one door, it can be entered through another.

There is no typical Jew-by-Choice. Converts come to Judaism for many reasons. Some may have felt spiritually or intellectually stifled in the religion into which they were born or raised. Others may have been raised "unchurched" and are looking for that spiritual ingredient which was missing in their early lives. Others may experience no religious "angst," but are pleasantly surprised to find that Judaism offers a view of God and holiness which they held personally for years, one for which they did not have a name.

The most common contemporary convert to Judaism is a non-Jew who is about to marry a Jew. While love between a Jew and a non-Jew is not sufficient reason to convert, it is often the chief motivating force to pursue a Jewish identity. This should not be surprising. As Judaism historically does not seek converts, the closest contact that many non-Jews have with Judaism is through their most personal and intimate of relationships.

Many elements within Judaism hold special significance for the Jew-by-Choice, especially the absolute monotheistic concept of God: Eternal, elemental, all-encompassing, fathomable, and, most of all, One. God is Partner in a sacred covenant-relationship with the Jewish people. A further attraction is Judaism's capacity to elevate and transform life's mundane moments into manifestations of holiness.

Coupled with these things is Judaism's emphasis on community and family life, on contributing to the larger world, on intense intellectual striving, and on attachment to a people who have survived exile, prejudice and atrocity for more than 4,000 years.

Each Jew-by-Choice is on a fascinating—and highly individual—spiritual quest. The path of each is unique, though there are some common threads. Typically, a candidate for conversion might initially approach a rabbi. In Judaism, a rabbi is not an intermediary between God and humankind. Rather, the rabbi is a teacher who transmits Jewish tradition and values. The rabbi also serves as a "gatekeeper" who sets the standards which must be embraced by those seeking to convert. Actual conversion is formalized through lengthy study, acceptance of ritual and commitment, and pledging fidelity to the Jewish people. After all this, the Jew-by-Choice acquires a Hebrew name. From that moment, Jewish law *(halakhah)* considers the convert to be fully Jewish. The inner transformation is so complete that it is even considered improper to ever again discuss that person's prior status as a convert, unless the individual initiates such a discussion. After conversion there is, under Jewish law, no difference between the Jew-by-Birth and the Jew-by-Choice; bringing up one's conversion would invade one's privacy and denigrate one's past. For that reason, the authors of the life-stories that follow are identified only by their Hebrew names, which they chose upon their conversion.

It is our hope that the stories in *Embracing the Covenant* will help people of all faiths and backgrounds understand why some people choose Judaism.

We hope that these stories will help those contemplating conversion to better understand the issues surrounding conversion. By discovering what others have wrestled with as they journeyed toward conversion, those considering conversion will have a clearer picture of what lies ahead.

Those who have already decided to convert will find in these stories ways to adjust or to connect to the Jewish community more easily by reading about the experiences of others who have already converted.

Often, the Jewish member of the family in a household in which there has been a conversion has difficulty understanding just what their loved one goes through during conversion. The process may mystify them since they may not understand their mate's deepest concerns. The following stories illuminate what Jews-by-Choice may be thinking and feeling, and especially their fears about the future and their anxiety about losing their former identity.

Finally, these stories can help rabbis and other Jewish institutional professionals who counsel Jews-by-Choice and their families.

While collecting these stories, it became increasingly clear that they addressed four main themes, around which this book was eventually organized:

- "The Search for God and Spirituality," stories about the pursuit of the Divine by Jews-by-Choice. God has called to them in a quiet, yet insistent Voice. Becoming a Jew is their way of answering that Call. In their stories, they write about their search for meaning and about Judaism quenching the thirst of their soul.

- "The Appeals of Judaism," accounts of Judaism's powerful

attractions for the convert. In many ways, these stories are a spiritual mirror for those born as Jews since they reflect Judaism's positive qualities.

• "Journeys to Judaism," which presents the many different paths which Jews-by-Choice have traveled on the road to conversion. Though they all end up at Judaism's doorstep, Jews-by-Choice arrive there from different points on the map, each with diverse life-experiences and with varied spiritual needs.

• "Turning Faith into Action," the last section, chronicles the inner transformation from "Jew-by-Choice" to "Jew." Here, converts speak of oppression in Eastern Europe during the Cold War, of redemption after the Holocaust, of relief from emotional distress.

Preceding and ending each section are "Gleanings," brief quotes from dozens of converts about their experiences and insights. These succinctly capture the converts' thoughts and emotions on a wide range of related issues. Through them, we hope to provide additional perspectives on converts and conversion.

Whether you were born a Jew, converted to Judaism, are thinking about converting, are close to someone who converted or just want to know more about conversion, we hope that these life-stories inform you about Judaism's beauty and richness and about those who, having listened to an ancient voice—and to the voice of their heart—have chosen Judaism.

—RABBI ALLAN L. BERKOWITZ
—PATTI MOSKOVITZ

SECTION I

The Search for
God and Spirituality

*Dearer to God than all of the Israelites who
stood at Mt. Sinai is the convert. Had the
Israelites not witnessed the lightning, thunder,
quaking mountain, and sounding trumpets
they would not have accepted the Torah. But
the convert who did not see nor hear any of
these things, came and surrendered himself to
God and took the yoke of heaven upon himself. Can anyone be dearer to God than such a
person?*

—TANCHUMA BUBER,
Lech Lecha 6:32A

EMBRACING GOD AND SPIRITUALITY

The Jewish tradition holds converts in high regard because of their devotion to God. Indeed, the Bible tells us that the Messiah will come from the line of King David, himself a descendant of Ruth, a Moabite who converted to Judaism. It is also said that the great sage, Hillel, who lived in the First Century of the Common Era, was descended from a convert.

Many converts are impressed by Judaism's understanding of God. In a famous Chasidic teaching, the question "Where is God?" is answered by, "Wherever we let God in." A complementary teaching suggests that the soul seeks to embrace God, *always*. The opportunity to feel nearer to God is a motivating factor in one's religious expression. How that connection with God is experienced is of great importance.

Judaism is not based on the premise that there is an intermediary or an intercessor between us and God. The person seeking the Holy through Judaism can heed the call of the soul directly. Common to many Jews-by-Choice is the sense that their connection with God is enhanced through Jewish religious expression.

Through the stories in this section, we can begin to understand the connection to God that many Jews-by-Choice seek. They speak about how open and accessible God is to them through Judaism, an opportunity which many converts had longed for throughout their lives.

To the Jew-by-Choice, the opportunity to approach God with questions and doubts may have extraordinary value. What may be most important may not be the answer itself, but rather the groping, the struggle, to find the answer since Judaism values, above all, the struggle itself. Jewish tradition is filled with examples of Jews struggling to understand God, even with examples of Jews challenging and confronting God. This time-honored rebelliousness started with Abraham, when he argued with God about Sodom and Gomorrah and raised questions about the morality of destroying human beings—even those who are evil. God accepted the questions and entered into the dialogue, saying, "If you will find me fifty righteous men, I will spare the cities." For the Jew-by-Choice, it is thrilling to be encouraged to wrestle with the Divine.

The Chasidic Rabbi Levi Yitzchak of Berditchev, who lived in the late eighteenth century, once interrupted his Yom Kippur prayers, demanding to know why God let the Jewish people suffer. The rabbi, who was holding God accountable, was struggling to answer the eternal question, "Where is God when good people suffer?" Judaism's answer is that God is found in our ability to persevere *despite* the trauma. But more noteworthy than the answer is the Jew's inherent *right* to even ask the question. It is this freedom to inquire and to doubt, and the recognition that God Who created human intellect is celebrated when we utilize our intellectual faculties, that so often appeal to Jews-by-Choice.

Judaism seeks to infuse the ordinary with sanctity. A Jewish blessing which speaks of God's presence in nature can be recited upon seeing a beautiful waterfall or a perfect rainbow. A Jewish blessing thanking God for the joyous moments in life can be recited upon hearing good news. When a Jew hears bad news, there is a blessing to remind us that there is order in the world despite moments of chaos. This reminder that God is forever present speaks to the soul of the convert. Judaism urges each of us to live a *meaningful* life, and the purpose of Jewish ritual is to lend daily meaning to our lives. Such welcoming of the Divine into our daily lives also appeals to Jews-by-Choice.

In the following stories, Jews-by-Choice tell how Judaism helped them bring God into their lives. These Jews-by-Choice let *us* in to their lives just as they "let God in" to their souls.

GLEANINGS

I generally fall short of achieving my ideals, but every day I start over. Every day I have the same goal: To lead a life that reflects God. Every day I start with the Barkhu, *the* Sh'ma, *the* V'ahavta, *and conclude with a silent prayer and* Oseh Shalom. *I have found a family, a way of life to hold me when I am feeling homesick for God.*

—HANNAH RUTH

The Sh'ma *declares the central belief of Judaism and of myself that God exists and that God is One. There is no need for any intermediaries between (wo)man and God; we can have a direct relationship with God. Like the Jewish people, I feel grateful to have a unique relationship with God—unique and special, but not in the sense that I am better than anyone else in their relationship with God. And I believe that we are here to make the world a better place to live because we are here.*

—ALISA CHAYA

Worshipping as a Jew releases something inside me that lets me think about God.   —SARAH RACHEL

Some Jewish rituals have posed huge questions for me and caused me to question why I even need religion:

I live a good life and I do good deeds, so why should I fast on Yom Kippur? Why should I celebrate the freedom of people who lived thousands of years ago? Why celebrate the giving of the Ten Commandments?

I don't have any black-and-white answers to these questions. I do have a Jewish answer. Fasting on Yom Kippur, for example, can help tune my soul to the life-giving force of the universe that we call God. Many rituals can teach us to give thanks for all that we have been given. On some days, I meditate and contemplate and argue these issues with myself. On other days, I just accept them and yield to their power and wisdom. —MICHAL

A PIECE OF TOAST
by Zakiya

A FEW WEEKS AGO, I WENT TO MY FIRST PASSOVER *Seder* (evening meal and ritual with which Passover begins). I was very nervous, not knowing the rituals or the Hebrew blessings very well, not knowing the people well. What if I looked stupid? What about my hair and clothes? What would I talk about? After all, it had been only ten months since I began to seriously explore Judaism.

The evening was wonderful. The wine was abundant, the food superb. Every person there was going through some kind of transition in their life, just as I was. Conversation wasn't difficult. It was a great evening.

Upon awakening the next morning, I knew I had the flu. After I got the kids off to school, I went back to bed. I thought of the delightful time I'd had the evening before and the new friendships that I'd made. It hadn't been so frightening, after all.

My stomach started hurting again. I was sure that if I had just one piece of toast, my stomach would settle and I would be cured.

Zakiya, a 42-year-old former Protestant, converted to
Judaism four years ago.

9

But I knew why there was no bread in the house, and that I had chosen to remove all leavened products from my home as required for the eight days of Passover. Yet, I wanted that bread and I began to obsess on why I couldn't have it.

I started thinking of the Passover story and how courageous our forefathers had been to have kept such unshakable faith in an unseen Power. Six hundred thousand people delivered from over 400 years in bondage in a strange, hostile land by believing in one God. God had chosen Moses to lead the Israelites to freedom. Moses occasionally argued with God, but ultimately obeyed Him. Miraculous things happened, just as God had told him they would.

Through Moses, God told the Jews what was expected of them:

> *This is what you shall do. This is what you shall not do. Do your best. I will make of you a great nation…You will remember who you are and what I have done for you. Tradition will make you strong of spirit and soul, and you and your children and your children's children will not forget…*

I also thought of my own journey. We all have a personal destiny that is ours alone. Is choosing another path disrespectful toward what my parents had wanted for me?

We all want good things for our children. We love them, cherish them, nurture them. We try to give them expectations they can meet, and encourage them when they don't. At some point, we realize that they are on their own personal journey, and that we will be remembered by the groundwork we laid and the traditions we gave them. They make their own choices and leave their mark on humanity.

I would want to tell my mother and my father, if he were here, that even though I have chosen a different path, it wasn't because they did anything wrong. I did it because they did so many things *right*. They instilled in me a special spirit, somewhat restless and unpredictable at times, that questions and digs for answers. It usually led me to difficult and frustrating routes, but also enabled me to make choices which I had to think about and for which I had to be responsible. It would have been easier so many times to do just the opposite, but that was not always the ethical thing to do.

That restless spirit often got me in hot water, but I had to do what I thought was correct and not make any excuses for my actions.

The ability to think for one's self is a great and precious gift for which I thank you, Mom and Dad. I want you to know that our God is the same.

Will embracing Judaism estrange me from my family? Will they understand my choice? Will I be able to set a new religious groundwork for my children? Can I establish traditions for them so they can remember who they are? Can I teach them that the easy way is not always the right way? Will they learn that the important messages in life are given, not by what you say, but by what you do?

My mind was exhausted. So many questions, and very few answers right now.

I no longer wanted that piece of toast. I didn't need it anymore.

The End

...and the beginning

THE CHOOSING ONES
by Omri

"Ki vanu vacharta" ("For You have chosen us")

—FROM THE HEBREW BLESSING OVER THE WINE

MY EDUCATION THUS FAR IN JUDAISM HAS BEEN exciting and enlightening. I have read many Jewish publications, and the phrase "The Chosen Ones" is still somewhat troublesome for me to accept. After everything I have read, it seems that the phrase should really be "The Choosing Ones"!

God had so many children in the world from whom to choose. But what made Abraham so special? What did he do to distinguish himself to show that he was worthy of God's blessing?

The *Midrash* (rabbinic commentary on the Bible) tells us that others rejected God, and then He *chose* the Jews. But what had they done to distinguish themselves from all others? Was it their righteous living or their suffering?

They are the ones who, when confronted with God, *chose* to accept God and chose to live by God's commandments. As a Jew–

Omri, a 39-year-old former Roman Catholic, converted to
Judaism eight years ago.

by-Choice, I know that, throughout history, choosing to be a Jew or to remain a Jew has been difficult. From the Exodus with Moses to war under King David to suffering in the Diaspora to the devastation of the Holocaust, they still *chose* to be Jews—and to remain Jews.

It is often said that "if you put two Jews into one room and ask them the same question, they'll have three opinions." I firmly believe that: The freedom this implies, the freedom to choose *my* beliefs, *my* worship, and *my* God, is what has made my choice to live as a Jew so meaningful.

As I learn more and more about Judaism and about Jews' luxury to question and argue, I am continually surprised that the Torah was ever completed and canonized since Jews so openly and fervently debate and bicker. But this is what I enjoy so very much about my new religious choice: The chance to be able to question and not to follow blindly.

> To reflect on *The Choosing Ones:*
> Who chooses—
> to engross oneself in the study of the *Torah*
> to quench one's thirst with the study of *Talmud*
> to honor and abide by the Commandments
> to choose the foundations of life as truth, justice, and peace
> to rest and pray on *Shabbat*
> to pray on *Rosh Hashanah*
> to fast on *Yom Kippur*
> to kindle the lights of *Hanukkah*
> to feast at the Seder on *Pesah*
> to weep on *Yom HaShoah*
> to mourn on *Tisha B'Av*
> to live the *Sh'ma*
> And "...to do justly, to love mercy, and to walk humbly with
>   God."

RED LIGHTNING
by Aharon

AS AN AIR TRAFFIC CONTROLLER STATIONED AT A small facility in Indiana, I enjoyed working the all-night shift. Those nights were invariably peaceful, interrupted only occasionally by light planes passing over to or from Indianapolis or other cities east or west. Sometimes I broke regulations and chatted briefly with a pilot, passing through that invisible barrier between authorized communications and human contact.

The airport beacon sat atop the control tower, alternately showing white and green, white and green, six times a minute. From a distance, the beacon's flashes of light seemed to say, "here...here...here..." to pilots. I felt as if I was in the very center of the universe. Sometimes I'd wave a silent farewell before passing them over to the next controller along their flight routes.

At the time, Kim and I were newlyweds, strangers to each other and to the Midwest. One night in late December, after the year's first heavy snowfall, we walked together near the banks of the Wabash. The sky was clear and calm. The moon was full and

Aharon, a 42-year-old former Catholic, converted to Judaism four years ago.

14

the stars had been washed clean. We held hands as we walked, our breath freezing in the cold night air. Neither of us had lived in the snow or cold before. We hadn't known the pristine quiet or hallowed stillness that can follow a storm. For us, it was a magical time. When we looked back toward the river from the edge of the path, our footsteps in the snow were silhouetted by the moonlight. The course we had taken was clear and easy to see. It was the last time we ever knew that luxury.

Late spring was the most interesting season to work. On many nights, I sat high in the darkness and watched thunderstorms approach from the northwest. They appeared first as silent, blood-red spikes of lightning against the black horizon. As they moved toward me, the color of the lightning gradually changed from red to gold. Sooner or later, I would hear the thunder rumbling and echoing in the distance. Then the wind would pick up, and leaves, dead since autumn, danced and skittered. Rain followed the wind and lightning followed the rain until earth and sky merged in darkness and light. Then, almost more suddenly than seemed possible, the storm was gone and the sky was clear and another flight called in to report as it passed through to an unknown destination.

Time has passed since then, and like the beacon calling out to those planes, the rabbi's sermon on the second morning of Rosh Hashanah touched me very deeply. "Late last year I invited a gentleman to speak to my Confirmation class," he said. "He was in the process of becoming a Jew-by-Choice. When he told the kids he wasn't converting for marriage or for any of the other usual reasons, their mouths literally dropped open. When he added that he kept kosher, lit Shabbat candles on Friday nights and attended synagogue, one of them said, 'You're more Jewish than I am!'

"Something very important happened that night. By the time class ended, they realized that Judaism didn't have to be a burden. It could give them wings. They saw that being Jewish made them special."

The rabbi challenged us in the new year to re-examine our relationship with Judaism; to find in it not the burden, but the honor; to share with our families, friends and neighbors, the joy of being Jews.

The rabbi did not reveal that it was I who had spoken to the class, that I had known within a few minutes after sitting down in the Introduction to Judaism course that I was about to discover a set of wings for my soul—and also place my feet more solidly on the ground than ever before. My certainty about that has only increased in the passing weeks and months.

Sometimes, late at night, I miss those old days in the tower when the night folded softly around me or when a storm passed over in its wild flight. I miss the mystery of it, the challenge, the beauty. I miss knowing the rules and being certain of them. Then I realize that when Kim and I looked back at our footsteps in the snow on that frozen December evening what we did not and could not know was that we had always been lost. We had only love to bind us, but no beacon to guide us, no set of instructions, no regulations, no plan for our marriage, no shared destination. There was red lightning in the moonlight, but neither of us saw it.

Storms of the human heart are not much different than those that split the night with thunder. Had we been prepared, we might have survived it. Maybe we could even have enjoyed it for its awesome power, beauty, and the potential it had to renew our love. One thing is certain: There will always be storms in the days and nights of human existence.

I love Judaism because it provides time-tested rules and a plan for reaching the most precious destination of my soul: profound love and peace. Through the Torah and its commandments, the rituals in home and synagogue, Judaism offers what I need to weather any storm of the heart, to find again that steady beacon of God's love and presence, and to hear Adonai's eternal voice saying, "I am here, I am here, I am here."

CONVERSION
by Simcha

I don't remember when it happened, really
When the sky changed color and the earth became more solid
Perhaps driving toward Jerusalem, the sun insistent,

Arguing about morality without God;
though the sky is silent, I said, we can still be good.
He laughed and said many clever things.

and suddenly it didn't matter anymore—the argument
or the heat or anything but the sun
under which there is nothing new.

—Or was it later that week, walking through the falling
Shabbat toward synagogue; David teaching the *Sh'ma* to a goy—
the syllables tumbling in my mouth like unfamiliar cherries—

Simcha, a 30-year-old former Roman Catholic, converted
to Judaism two years ago.

A commonplace to God. Millions of moments like this
back and forward forever in time.
At the time I hardly noticed—

It was summer and I was wrestling with love
it was busy and hot and I hardly noticed

———————

I remember my father explaining the world;
an orange in his right hand, an apple revolving in his left.
His arms drew the paths of the planets

And it all seemed clear. When sometimes I would cry
about the world of pain, he would explain
that things were better than they had been—

The Enlightenment, sanitation, antibiotics;
people living longer than ever before—
Certainly there were some...

the superstitious, the uneducated
who clung to the old ways but
the writing was on the wall and in the books of Marx

I was comforted; Dad understood the world,
the sun kept rising. The Egyptian sarcophagi
in the hall looked calmly into forever

not meeting my gaze
and the house was still.

———————

Anne Frank Chaim Potok Primo Levi—Bertrand Russell—I
argued with the chaplain at school who was young and quite

good looking.
Had a period of piety at ten, because of Bach—

but it was all so hellishly anemic the air was thin,
and reminded me of my grandmother—
her potpourri, her still lives,
her resignation and her brandy-breath bitterness

Save me save me
Out of the depths I call you

———————

II
They fell into my hands—books, poems, Jewish ideas.
Jocelyn, friend of my heart, back from Israel, explaining *Sabra*—
I went to Italy to study Italian and love the art—

But the Madonnas were painted by artists who were slaves;
the Bridge of Sighs a path to dungeons and screams
monuments to dead emperors and a hundred ghastly wars;

in Paris, a man held a sign saying, "I have nothing
but my hunger."
And in the plenitude of lack

all around, the child prostitutes—the stones on which the Nazis
        walked
—the young needled and poisoned;
all of history weighed down on me like a marble slab.

Always only this?—the endless cycle of cruelty, washed down
        with wine;
the sickening dance of power—most people crushed;
The others built churches and patronized art

Stony with soundless grief for weeks, suddenly it was revealed
to me
nothing   nothing   nothing
separated me from the man with the empty sign

the woman with the empty bottle, the dirty gypsy kid
except what could be bought
which is nothing

we are all one
and so separate.
I noticed and was torn apart

———————

III
At first the old words were utterly mysterious
I was lost in the *siddur* and other people's prayers—
When the rhythms became familiar I hardly noticed

that the gentle loveliness of *Shabbat*
changed the rhythm of the week; soul
rocks itself to peace

and the righteous rage of the prophets
burns soul to life again. Evening and morning, another day;
and now rage burns and I am not consumed.

———————

IV   *A Prayer*

Blessed Lord, Ruler of the Universe
Thank you for my mother singing lullabies and her love
and for my father telling me it could all be different

Thank you for that Jerusalem heat
and for David's words and his love
and for revelation in rage in Rome

Help me be one of these people.
I am deeply blessed.

Amen

GLEANINGS

I went through a period in my life pursuing nagging theological/existential questions. I fed my intellect's desire to know, but left all spirituality aside. Now, practicing Judaism has become the means for uniting my intellectual questions and my spiritual yearnings.

—NAOMI

The other night, I heard myself saying exactly what I feel at a Shabbat potluck that I attended. As I did, I said to myself, "Yes. This is what it's all about." To another convert, I said, "How can we look at the life and love around us and within us and not feel a sense of awe and reverence for the Creator of all of this? Every day I give thanks to the life-giving force of the universe, the force that we Jews call God."

—MICHAL

God is still awesome and beyond human comprehension. But to me, God is now also a friend. Someone to talk to, argue with, get angry at, question, cry with, share with, listen to, consult, wrestle with and, finally, to love.

This changing concept of God is indescribable; my responsibilities to this God are overwhelming at times. At the same time, the joy and anticipation of a growing, continuing rela-

tionship with an approachable, accepting God will lead me to more searching, questioning and learning.
—DAVIDA ORA

I have made a firm decision about God and this life I'm living right now. I believe in God. No, I love God, and my life, and my family. The decision to convert to Judaism has put my mind so much at ease. For years, I have wondered how I fit into the scheme of things, especially religiously. Now, I have this incredible peace of mind. I can't find words deep enough to express the exhilaration I feel.
—HADASSAH

SECTION II

The Appeals of Judaism

The Torah was given in public, openly, in a free place. Had it been given in the Land of Israel, the Israelites could have said to the nations of the world: "You have no share in it." But since it was given in the wilderness, in a free place for all, everyone wishing to accept it could come and do so.

—FROM THE MEKHILTA
(a collection of rabbinic folk-tales from the first and second centuries, C.E.)

EMBRACING THE APPEALS OF JUDAISM

Upon converting to Judaism, one adopts a relationship, commitment and identification with a new belief system and a new people. Some Jews-by-Choice discover new bonds and a stronger sense of personal identity which had previously eluded them.

Others are attracted by the importance that Judaism places on family or find *Shabbat*, the Jewish Sabbath, to be of overriding importance to them since in our busy world, where hours filled with meaning are rare, the idea of an entire day of rest, one devoted to reflection and communion with the holy is compelling and attractive. Still others discover a new inner strength and tenacity by emulating those qualities exhibited by the Jewish people throughout their 4,000 years of history. Or they may enter into a partnership with God in repairing the world and helping it achieve a holy state. As the prophet Isaiah (42:7) says, "To take the prisoner out of the prison-house, to free the captive, to open the blind eye..." For someone choosing Judaism, such actions raise life to an idealistic venture; they let us be the true partner of God.

Converts are also attracted to Judaism's emphasis on per-forming acts of lovingkindness. There is a love of all creation, and a celebration of every moment. Fulfilling God's commandments, or *mitzvot*, is viewed as a ladder to God which enhances one's life and makes firm one's steps along the way.

And finally, converts are attracted to Judaism's emphasis on freedom of the mind and will. Judaism stresses learning and study and encourages intellectual and spiritual growth and inquiry. One is not told to blindly accept a doctrine, but to study it to deter-mine its validity.

By adopting these qualities of Judaism, Jews-by-Choice report that they have found a place within the cosmos and with-in the Jewish People.

GLEANINGS

My friends and family have all been very excited about my conversion to Judaism, as a spiritual home was really the missing link in my "personhood." The decision to convert is one of the best decisions I ever made. I am at peace with my feelings about God, life, knowledge, love, and death. I also feel more at ease with what is expected of me in this world. Being a Jew has completed my life and brought with it so many beautiful and awesome things. It is something no one can ever take from me.

—HADASSAH

Why in the world did I want to convert? There are many reasons: Family and the opportunity of transmitting tradition, ideology and way of life to others is important to me. The journeys of the Jews are amazing. The Jewish way of thinking and the kindness, fairness and common sense Judaism offers. The beauty of Shabbat. *The concept of* Tzedakah, *of helping others. The sound of the shofar, the ram's horn blown on* Rosh Hashanah, *the Jewish New Year. The simple blessings for simple wonders. I could go on and on. Actually, I will—in my life!*

—ORA

Judaism strengthens me in times of crisis. It provides the sense of community and belonging for which Judaism is uniquely known. I feel a profound connection with a nation and a history and culture which remembers a glorious past and anticipates a redeeming future. Judaism will show me the way to become a moral and holy person.

—Sarah Rachel

Judaism helped me validate my need for joy and pleasure in life. It helped me feel the love of God. It helped me understand life. It helped me trust life, and it reaffirmed my sense of destiny.

Because of Judaism, I am proud of who I am. Because of it, I understand my place in life and my role in this universe.

—Rafi

A LETTER TO MY PARENTS: WHY I AM BECOMING A JEW

by Nafshiya

IN A FEW DAYS, I WILL PARTICIPATE IN A CEREMONY that dates back millennia: The *mikveh*. When I emerge from this ritual bath, I will be spiritually renewed with a new identity and will have officially converted to Judaism.

As I approach this moment, I am aware that you, my parents, may have questions, concerns, and emotional reactions to my new identity as a Jew. Indeed, during my Jewish studies over the past months, even my Jewish friends have asked me why and how I have reached this decision. "After all," they explained, "anti-Semitism is a reality. To become a Jew is to be connected to a history often filled with pain and struggle."

I did not come to this decision hastily. Years of soul-searching, pondering and deliberating have gone into it. In Judaism, I have found the values and traditions that I have searched for.

Nafshiya, a 38-year-old who was raised with no formal religion, converted to Judaism two years ago.

Before I continue, I wish to express a vital message to you, one to keep with you always in your hearts and in your minds: You are my parents, and I love you. Your love and guidance have been, as they are today, a continual source of strength and security for me. This strength is a blessing, for which I will be eternally grateful. You have shown me the kind of love a daughter needs if she is to realize her true self and make the choices that are right for her. So let there be no doubt: I am making the right choice and I need you to know that becoming Jewish does not mean I am leaving my roots. On the contrary, I'm adding to them. Even though I will be a child of Abraham and Sarah—and a daughter of Israel—I will always be your little girl.

Deciding to become Jewish feels completely natural and exciting, although I do not believe that this is the way for everyone.

I'd like to explain some of the aspects of Judaism that particularly appeal to me. First is the task of the Jewish People: *Tikkun olam,* "repairing the world." This decree obliges Jews to live in ways that will improve the state of the world and help bring about the Messianic Age, the highest ideal of peace, brotherhood and love. This will not occur unless we engage in *gemilut hasadim,* "deeds of lovingkindness," and closely follow the laws given to us by God. These 613 commandments or *mitzvot* in the Five Books of Moses (the Torah) include everything from how to conduct business to what to do for a wounded animal. They address how, when and what to eat. There is even a law requiring placing a parapet around one's roof so that someone working on it won't fall and injure himself. Being mindful of these *mitzvot* lets us contribute profoundly to the world's betterment.

This is not to say that Jews alone have a stake in the world's repair. All people can join together to make the world a better place, each in his or her own way, with their particular skills and knowledge.

Another significant facet of Judaism is its holidays, festivals and days of remembrance. In keeping with the Jewish emphasis on cycles, tradition and history, the calendar is full of certain days to help us to reflect on our place in the world. In the past few months, I have observed several holidays which have brought me closer to my new faith. Last March, for example, I attended a *seder*, the ritual festive meal of Passover. Passover celebrates Moses leading the Israelites out of slavery in Egypt over 3,000 years ago. As a Jew, I will tell my children this story so they can tell it to theirs. Thus, these stories and traditions will never cease.

Another memorable event I recently attended was *Yom HaShoah*, the Day of Remembrance of the Holocaust. The commemorative service for this memorial day was observed collectively by several local synagogues, with representatives from churches and other community groups also participating. The service also featured one of the "Schindler's List" survivors. Although the images evoked of suffering during the Holocaust were painful, they also reaffirmed Jews' strength and resolve to survive. It made me proud to be among those who now carry on God's work, who continue to survive and prosper, and who will carry the memory of this sorrow to future generations.

Some holidays in particular will require adjustments for us, particularly in December. For about the same time you'll be celebrating Christmas, I'll be lighting the menorah as I observe Hanukkah, the holiday which celebrates the victory of the Jewish Maccabees over the Greco-Syrians. These changes may be awkward at first, but I hope all my friends and family will approach them with a healthy curiosity and embrace this opportunity to learn together.

Anyone who knows me knows that history and geography have never been my best subjects. When I started studying them during the courses about Judaism that I recently finished, I thought, "Oh dear! I'll never be able to make sense of all this— 4,000 years of history taking place in parts of the world I know so little of!" Yet, I forged ahead despite my trepidation. My teacher told me stories and facts, gave me history books, maps, tapes and novels. Slowly, steadily, everything began to fall into place. Unlike my previous history studies, the Jewish story assumed a personal significance that made learning it natural and enjoyable. This was clearly another affirmation of my newly chosen identity.

Judaism began around the year 2,000 B.C.E. (Before the Common Era) with the Age of the Patriarchs—Abraham, Isaac, and Jacob. Abraham and his wife, Sarah, considered the first family of Judaism, broke away from the pagan tribes of ancient Sumer and embraced the one true God. In an act of absolute devotion, Abraham was even willing to sacrifice his own son, Isaac, to demonstrate his obedience to God. This was only a test of Abraham's faith. God prevented the sacrifice and, by doing so, declared His protection and love for the People of Israel throughout all generations. The covenant that God made with Abraham continues to bind Jews to God, and God to Jews.

Moving through thousands of years of history and into the modern world, I learned much about the land called Israel, and how it came to be a nation in our time. In the late nineteenth century, a Jewish journalist and lawyer, Theodor Herzl, convened a gathering of Zionists in Basel, Switzerland. This First Zionist Congress, as it became known, envisioned a place where all Jews would be safe from persecution and enjoy religious freedom. This vision was realized in 1948, with the creation of the State of Israel. As a Jew, I have pledged to work for Israel's continued existence and its quest for a full and absolute peace.

Everything I have learned—each holiday, feast, story or day of remembrance—has significance for me. I am connected to its history, which I am anxious to share with friends and family.

My beloved parents, if you visit my Jewish home on a Friday evening, you will see the *Shabbat* candles burning brightly. I hope you will join us as we recite the *berachot*, the blessings, which celebrate the kindling of these lights and the drinking of the wine. After a blessing over the bread, we can all enjoy a hearty Sabbath meal. I won't be eating bacon when I come for breakfast anymore, but please come over for lox and bagels, anytime!

Love and *L'chaim*,
Nafshiya

SOURCE OF ALL LIFE
by *Yaakova*

SHALOM.

Blessed are You, Source of all life, who has made me a Jew. On this day of my *mikveh* (ritual bath used in the conversion ceremony), I pray that I am worthy of the privilege of sharing the destiny of the people of Israel.

How I have become a Jew is easier to explain than *why* I have taken this path. Jewish life meets my needs for community and spirituality, and touches me in a way that no other religious fellowship has. My deep faith in the Infinite One is strengthened by Jewish views of God. The *Sh'ma*, the proclamation of God's oneness, calls Israel to hear the truth of unity. I believe that nothing rivals the truth of one holy source of Being.

My maternal grandmother once told me that anyone claiming that the path to salvation was owned by any church was just plain wrong. She gave me permission to be true to myself. In doing so, she gave me permission to become a Jew.

The joy of *Shabbat* was one of the first lights (pun intended)

*Yaakova, a 38-year-old African-American raised as a
Unitarian, converted to Judaism two years ago.*

that attracted me to Judaism. My college roommate practiced modern Orthodox Judaism, and I felt that I had come home when I was a guest at her table on Friday nights. *Shabbat* remains at the center of my own religious practice. Then I stop the week's activities and refresh myself with prayer, song and meditation, and a better than ordinary Friday night meal.

Hanukhat Habayit, the affixing of the *mezuzah* (ritual object affixed to the doorway of Jewish homes) on our door; the *Tu B'Shevat seder*, the mystically-inspired meal for the celebration of the Jewish Arbor Day; and *menorah* lighting during *Hanukkah* are among other rituals I've enjoyed. I've learned more about religious life and about human nature by reading the ancient stories and by bringing the experience of our foreparents to my 1990s life.

Jewish education is an ongoing process for me. It ranges from the sublime of study with an Introduction to Judaism class to my ridiculous wish to dress up as Queen Esther for Purim, a holiday of revelry which celebrates the rescue of Persian Jews from near-annihilation in the fourth century B.C.E. The introductory course in Biblical Hebrew that I took allows me to follow along in the *siddur*, the prayerbook, and to speak and sing some of the service. My rabbi has helped me greatly in my studies.

I hope that you will all join in my *simcha*, my day of joy, and that I might receive your blessings for my life as a new member of the people, Israel.

A JEW OF THE PRESENT AND FUTURE

by Yosef

TO ME, JUDAISM IS LIKE A BREATH OF NEW LIFE. IT IS as though, religiously, I have been rescued from a storm. I grew up Roman Catholic and was an altar boy during my childhood. Even into my teenage years, I became disappointed with aspects of the religion. Confession was one of those disappointments. Why couldn't I talk to God without an intermediary? As a Catholic, such a thought was considered a sin. I did not enjoy being told that I would burn in Hell if I did not follow all the rules. I became uneasy with the threats of my religion. Believing that religion should be loving, supportive and caring, not demeaning, unfair or unkind, I became a non-practicing Catholic.

This brings me to Judaism. My Jewish experience began nine years ago when I was invited by a friend to a *Shabbat* dinner. Lighting the Sabbath candles introduced me to the joys of the faith. The family unity in the blessings of the wine and challah

Yosef, a 29-year-old former Roman Catholic, converted to
Judaism two years ago.

made me feel closer to God and close to others in ways that I had previously not experienced. At *Hanukkah*, I learned the meaning and the symbols of the holiday, especially the miracle of the oil lasting for eight days, and the story of the Jews' courage during their war for religious freedom against the Greco-Syrians was intriguing and inspiring. In April, I enjoyed reading the Passover story in the *Haggadah*, the book that is read during the *seder*. I also enjoyed feeling the same joy of freedom as my new-found Jewish family. The story of the Exodus from slavery in Egypt over 3,000 years ago showed the strength and courage of the Jewish people.

I continued to explore the feelings evoked by these stories and holidays by involving myself in more observances. On *Rosh Hashanah*, the Jewish New Year, and on *Yom Kippur*, the Day of Atonement, I attended services and was welcomed with open, loving and caring arms by those around me. This was a feeling that I craved. I felt part of the community and close to God, even though the Hebrew language was foreign to me. I needed these feelings of comfort, acceptance and closeness, especially since I came from a dysfunctional family.

To me, Judaism was a "God-sent" atmosphere, an angel-covered path to a religiously fulfilling life. My connection to Judaism is more than emotion. It is real life. Jews have been oppressed and persecuted, yet they have survived. They—and now I—are here stronger than ever. My childhood was the same. I was abused and oppressed. But somehow, like the Jews, I survived. Jews have survived by believing in God, Torah and themselves. The Jewish people have endured in spite of everything, and so have I.

Now, I am Jewish! What a wonderfully exciting time for me! I feel as though I have always been a Jew because of the similarities between my life and the lives of the Jews of the past. I can now be a Jew of the present and the future. And hopefully, I can change the world a little through love, kindness, support, understanding and Torah.

"TURNING" AND GROWING
by Yonaton

SITTING IN SERVICES THIS YEAR AND SINGING BEAUTIFUL
Hebrew songs as we celebrated *Shavuot*, the holiday which commemorates the giving of the Torah at Mount Sinai, made me consider again some of the elements of Judaism and the synagogue
service which have attracted me. I am drawn toward many things,
including the sense of community, the emphasis on active participation, the opportunity for contemplation and questioning, the
belief in the purposefulness, order, and obligations of our lives,
and the incredible vitality and resilience of the tradition and of
those who pass it on.

It is now nearly two and a half years since I started coming
to Friday night services at this synagogue with Joyce, then a good
friend and now my fiancee. Initially, I came out of curiosity, com-
panionship and a desire to learn more about a tradition and religion to which I had had some exposure as an undergraduate.

I started attending quite often, and more and more liked the
island of rest and contemplation which that hour gave me amid

Yonaton, a 27-year-old raised with no formal religion,
converted to Judaism two years ago.

40

all the pressures, mindless routine and hectic rush of the week. I valued the service's emphasis on stepping back to behold the wonder of the world, on giving thanks for that wonder, on asserting our responsibility to better the world.

I also was attracted by Judaism's emphasis on action, rather than on faith or dogma. The *Shabbat* service, and the whole concept of a Sabbath of rest, serves only to stress the importance of being actively engaged during the rest of the week. This is one of the things I like most about Judaism: A commitment to it does not consist of a creed, "This is what I believe" (and have no need to know more about), but rather a pledge to learn and to keep learning, to do one's own questioning and interpreting, and to apply one's knowledge accordingly in practical ways.

More than two years ago, Joyce and I first sat down and had a long talk about values, religion and how we look at the world. Surprisingly (to me at the time, anyway, given our different religious backgrounds), we found that our views were really quite similar. We both had a tremendous belief in the supreme importance of family; we both valued intelligence and learning, optimism, responsibility and the importance of making a difference in our life and work. As for more specifically spiritual beliefs, we both felt wonder for the natural world and saw some larger force behind it. Neither of us felt comfortable putting a face or gender on that force, but Joyce put a religious name to it, whereas I did not. What to her was God was, to me, nature or the "order-of-things" or simply the beauty and pattern of the world.

In my thoughts about the meaning of taking on something as new and significant as a Jewish identity, a sense of continuity with my past has been very important. One of the central bases of my decision to convert to Judaism is a conviction that what I am doing does not involve a fundamental shift away from the values with which I grew up. No matter how much may have attracted me to Judaism, I could not have converted had this meant rejecting my family. This is not to say that I do not realize that I am making a big change, or that I am ignoring that my conversion may seem strange or foreign to my family. They may justly wonder why, given my entire lack of religious background, I now choose to join a religion. If Joyce and I felt so similar in so many ways to begin with, clearly most of the values we share are not specific to religion—and certainly not to one particular religion—so why do I need to convert?

What I have found in synagogue over the past several years has not been simply a feeling of being welcomed and accepted, but also a real sense of belonging. Reading the prayers of the service, singing in the choir, talking with new friends after services on Friday nights, I have gained a new community. My presence and participation were welcomed from the beginning. In fact, only a few weeks ago someone I have known quite well since my early days at the temple said, upon hearing I hoped to convert soon, "Really? I never knew you weren't Jewish!" My motivation to convert is deeply internal: I feel that I belong in Judaism and I want to express that identity.

Judaism imposes a sense of order and framework on the world, an order in which I belong and to which I can identify, just as I belong to the Jewish community of worshippers. I have found that, in Judaism, it is really impossible to separate the sense of individual spiritual fulfillment from the importance of community.

It is also important, however, to consider facets of becoming Jewish which are less easily dealt with. Anti-Semitism is not an abstract concept when you leave home each morning and see "Federov is a Yid" scrawled across the wall, as I did while living in Moscow last summer as a student. Jews' experience in America is the exception, not the rule, and it is crucial (if sobering) for those of us living here to have reminders like the Holocaust Memorial Museum in Washington, which I will visit in a few months.

How is someone like me to react to the Holocaust? The

realms of loss and suffering are so far beyond anything I have known that it seems almost wrong or presumptuous for me to claim that I can know Judaism "from the inside." Then again, I do not think this issue is unique to those people who are now choosing Judaism; even for many born-Jews of my generation, the Holocaust must seem alien, yet must be confronted. It gives all Jews a heavy responsibility: To continue the traditions for which others died, to ensure that the memory of their murders is not forgotten, and to devote our energies to making sure no such event will happen again.

Given that I was not born Jewish, is it responsible voluntarily to bequeath to my children and grandchildren the threat of anti-Semitism? To answer this, I pose another question: Is it not naive to believe that anyone, from any culture or religion, is forever free from the dangers of persecution? Certainly, Judaism has received more than its share of hatred and discrimination. But what I chose, and what I will bequeath to future generations, is not the hatred and persecution. I am making my choice fully aware of them, but I am also asserting how much I deplore them, and that I am willing to combat them any way I can.

As I choose a vibrant, positive tradition, I also commit myself to work for freedom, tolerance, justice and understanding. I realize that if such virtues fail, I may be more vulnerable.

But I cannot let this stand between me and what I gain.

Jewish tradition is giving me a strong basis to engage with the world. Emphasizing turning and growing outward while drawing sustenance from inner roots is one of Reform Judaism's greatest strengths. Much as I admired the persistence, in spite of all odds, of the Jewish community in Prague, where I recently attended a *Shabbat* service, my dominant impression was of a closed group that had little concern with the wider world. One of the central thrusts of Reform Judaism is to understand the importance of making contributions to society at large.

One aspect of Judaism which I particularly plan to follow is living a life of study. I have gained enormously from my lessons with my teacher. The sharing of knowledge, enthusiasm, warmth and insight have truly been wonderful experiences. I look forward to continuing my involvement at the synagogue by participating in scholastic, musical, social, and religious activities.

BEING GOD'S WITNESS
by Renatya

ON MY WAY TO ELEMENTARY SCHOOL IN THE OLD
Town of Bratslava, Czechoslovakia, was a passage which led into
some deep space in the ground. Strange things happened there.
Scary, strange-looking people with tall black hats, long black
coats, and funny-looking hair disappeared into the hole, spent
some time below, then reappeared. A few minutes after they
disappeared into the ground, you could hear unusual, medieval-
sounding songs.

My schoolmates and I were fascinated by the whole scene.
It was very difficult for us, being raised in a communist society
with absolutely no religion, to understand what the passageway
was all about. When we asked adults about it, we were told that it
was dangerous to go there, and if somebody from the school saw
us there, we would be in big trouble. Of course, that just made us
spend even more time there, but those people never talked to us
to let us know what their secret was about.

I now believe this was the burial place of a Hasidic rabbi.

Renatya, 28 years old and raised with no formal religion,
converted two years ago.

Growing up in a communist society, sheltered completely from the surrounding world, gave me no opportunity to find out what was outside the Iron Curtain. Being a strict atheist, understanding that only "weak" people believed in God, fully believing in Darwinian evolution, trusting that Brezhnev knew what he was doing—those were the basic conditions of becoming a good student. And that's what most of us wanted: To be good students and good patriots, and to save our country from decadent capitalism. Forbidden books were burned. No contacts were allowed with the outside world; and adults were terrified to talk about "the old days."

Upon entering high school, I began to have doubts about the whole system. By the time I entered the university, I knew that something was wrong. Being able to travel around the world with the committee which I had formed with a few of my schoolmates as part of "International Physicians for the Prevention of Nuclear War" let me have more information than ever before. At a conference in Hiroshima, I met a doctor from Boston, who became a close friend and introduced me to Judaism. As time went by, I realized that most of my best friends were Jewish. I became even more interested in Judaism.

One year after I finished medical school, my best friend, Natasha, invited me to spend the summer with her in Berkeley, California. There, I met Paul, my husband, and I decided to belong to the Jewish community there. We got married in a civil ceremony, then began attending an "Introduction to Judaism" class together. The more I studied about Judaism, the more it interested me. After finishing the class, I took lessons with a private tutor who taught me in greater depth the history, writings and observances of the Jewish people. My conversion process would have taken longer if not for Paul, who encouraged me on my journey.

Being raised as an atheist, I had a difficulty accepting the idea of an all-powerful God. Does such a God really exist?

For thousands of years, people have attempted to provide a satisfactory answer. Unlike our ancient forefathers, we neither hear nor see God. But whether or not there is a supernatural power, I believe that the world can be made divine and morally and spiritually pure by elevating humanity closer to the Holy Image.

In the Book of Isaiah, God says to the Jews, "You are my witnesses, I am the Lord." And as the sages say, "When we are His witnesses, He is the Lord. When we neglect being His witnesses, He is not our Lord." These words are very important. Only if we accept the task of being witness to God's moral law on earth will the thought of God have the capacity to affect the world.

Judaism is a faith of deeds and concrete efforts intended to instill equity and compassion in this world. Judaism begins with the community, with the past, with tradition. Each Jew is part of a big family, and despite all of Judaism's diversity in belief, each Jew knows that he or she belongs to each other.

"To Life!" A simple idea which strongly suggests a basic principle of Judaism: Not only what to believe, but how to live even before believing exists. The principle offers counsel on how to live in this world, not in the world to come: Enjoy the gratification of this life. Ask "why?" in happy times, when blessings are yours and life is joyful. Try not to pay too much attention to life's negative aspects.

Judaism is about learning. And knowledge gives the power not only to be clever, capable and bright, but also to be kind, good, considerate, generous. The power of wisdom makes us think differently and allows us to live differently, to commit ourselves to acting in a holy way in our day-to-day lives.

The question for me is not "Why should I be Jewish." The question is, "How can I be sincerely humane?" For *me*, being Jewish is the best way to be a human being. In this way, the question of whether God exists almost solves itself.

GLEANINGS

I mainly converted to Judaism for spiritual reasons, and was pleasantly surprised to find the friendship and community spirit that went along with it. It was like being a member of a big family with caring friends and an invitation to a whole new lifestyle. I love every minute of being Jewish. It has been the greatest thing to happen to me.

—Hannah

I came to my conversion while being divorced. At some point, I realized that part of my sorrow in Robert's decision to leave was a loss of my Jewishness, my Jewish family. Although I couldn't hold Robert to a marriage he no longer wanted, I could retain part of that experience by converting and by joining the larger Jewish family.

—Hannah Ruth

I am not the only one in my family who converted to Judaism. My daughter became a Jew-by-Choice over fifteen years ago. Some years later, my wife made the decision to become a Jew. Not long after that, I decided to convert. There is now a happiness among us that is quite difficult to put into words. We have a contentment that I never experienced previously. The greeting of "Shalom" has much more meaning to me than

"hello." It binds Jew to Jew. You are with a friend immediately; there is this common bond.
　　　　　　　　　　　　　　—Ze'ev

After reading and hearing so much about anti-Semitism, one would think that I would forget about converting. On the contrary, the more I learn about Jews and their way of life, the greater my desire to be one. I guess this is due partly to my admiration for them, for they have suffered so much and are yet so strong and proud of their identity, especially in times of trouble and perils. There seems to exist a unity, a bond, among these people.
　　　　　　　　　　　　　　—Adina Yaffa

When I began to study about Judaism, I was amazed that Jews dare to question and discuss everything!
　　　　　　　　　　　　　　—Davida Ora

SECTION III

Journeys to Judaism

Whosoever seeks to be converted should be accepted. Do not impugn the motives of gerim [converts]. Perhaps they come for the sake of heaven.

—*Rav,*
founder of the Academy at Sura,
3rd century, C.E.

EMBRACING THE JOURNEY

Just as a river may flow and flow and eventually reach the sea, so, too, may a searching soul eventually find a home. To a Jew-by-Choice, the path to Judaism may have begun long ago and in a far-distant place. The course of the journey may have been rocky and difficult, winding and obscure. For some, it meant leaving family and friends, finding new paths and making new trails. For others, it was a gentle continuation of something they glimpsed from afar in their childhood, something which seemed vaguely familiar and warm. For still others, the passage was storm-tossed and tumultuous, causing wrenching changes in their lives and in the lives of others around them. For all, the journey was life-transforming.

Again and again, we have heard stories of such life-passages from those who have become Jews. These people do not have a common religious denominator nor do they come from similar homes or backgrounds. Rather, each is unique since there are as many 'stories' as there are individuals. And though the destination of each convert may be the same, each travels a path which is highly personal.

For just as it is written that there are 600,000 letters in the Torah—one for each Jewish soul which came out of bondage in Egypt—so, too, each soul has a different story and approaches God in his or her own way, a way that speaks to that soul as could no other path or journey.

GLEANINGS

I had an experience which affected me strongly. An older lady at a nursing home which I visit was speaking of a man she didn't like very much. She said to me in a very derogatory way, "Do you think he's a Jew?," her mouth snarling as if she were swearing or talking about a Satanic killer.

I calmly replied, "I haven't the slightest idea if he's Jewish or not, but I am."

I felt so proud. At that moment, I realized that the Jews really are my people.

—Soer

Robert's mother was skeptical of his attraction to "shiksas," but after a dinner or two at her home, she said, "You're all right. You have a Jewish heart!" And it is true. The covenant is written in my heart. As a Jew, I am whole.

—Hannah Ruth

Those who go through the conversion process are generally self-less individuals who bring to the religion new perspectives, a strong interest and wonderful intentions. They are also, in many ways, still babes in the woods, requiring guidance.

Upon finishing my conversion class, I felt a huge sense of accomplishment and pride. But alas, I did not magically "feel" Jewish as I had hoped. A new category seemed to appear. Whereas in the past, there were "Jews" and "non-Jews," I was now faced with the category of "Jew-by-Choice." It was almost like being between a rock and a hard space, sometimes feeling as I didn't really fit in anywhere.

—CHAVA

As a Jew, I am happier and more myself than I have ever been. Judaism provides a context and structure which allows me to be myself, to accept my depths. It makes it okay to be different. In becoming a Jew, I have found what was always right under my nose. I've found my heart, my soul, my life.

—ARIELLA CHAYA

Did I really want to "join" a religion? What would that mean for me? How could I become part of a religion that believes in God when I don't know if I believe in God! But all the questions and doubts could not stop the strength I felt growing inside me. The thought of becoming Jewish gave me strength! It made me feel spiritual and proud! Where was this coming from? I can't say, but I knew that I wanted to do it. This part of my journey is the most difficult to describe because it is pure emotion, flowing in turbulent streams in rainbow colors. But it brought me to Judaism.

—MALKA ELISHEVA

FINDING A JEWISH MEMORY

by Sarah

I wandered
with soul thirsting
and heart bursting...
looking...
for a city to build my home.

I wandered
through a desert filled...
with mirages
wells that were empty
a chatter and clicking of mouths
dry and swollen...
Where is the city?
I want to build my home.

Sarah is a 48-year-old former Christian who converted
eight years ago.

I wandered
tired and discouraged
eyes red with tears and despair
feet broken and swollen
a heart heavy with yearning
I walked through pages of faith and God
and yet where is the city?
I want to build my home.

I wandered restless
without the comfort of home and nest
empty and without hope.
My soul from a cavern place
cried out...
echoing
screaming
pleading
for the city to build my home.

God in mercy and love
led me to Jerusalem
took me from my wandering
in the desert of my own emptiness
and gently placed me
in the city
a place that was always my home.

It is Hanukkah, and my first anniversary as a Jew-by-Choice, time for me to reflect on where I am as a Jewish person. I wish I could say I have arrived or discovered some sense of being Jewish. I told a friend recently that I feel less Jewish now than when I convert-ed. She said that isn't surprising since it is not unusual for even Jews to feel alien in their own tradition. Perhaps it is because as a

40-year-old divorced woman it is very difficult for me to connect with a community that is so focused on family. Perhaps, being single and being Jewish means to find myself without an ethnic Jewish identity while simultaneously trying to connect with Jewish men.

Often, someone will mutter something to me in Yiddish, and I have no idea what they are talking about. I am missing a Jewish memory. It is somehow my task to build a Jewish identity that is part of the larger whole, but also reflects my unique experience. It is a task that has, at times, been discouraging. But when I attend synagogue and hear the music and become part of the service, I know I am home.

My journey to Judaism is a journey to Jerusalem inside myself. My earliest memory is a sense of searching, of trying to find a place for myself. I intuitively knew that God had something to do with it, but finding God, a God that makes my heart sing and my feet dance, took me 38 years.

How can a Jew be caught in a gentile body? One could answer the question from a variety of philosophical positions, but I had to wander and spin through several religious traditions to find the answer inside myself.

My mother, a child bride of 15, was a mother by age 16. She always had a religious sensibility about her, but not in any traditional sense. It was a psychic and intuitive connection with her environment that led to visions and religious experiences which often did not have a name. She was wandering in her own kind of desert.

Somehow, I never was satisfied religiously. There was always a part of me that felt starved—and empty. I was baptized as a Presbyterian, irregularly went to Sunday School, and attended a United Protestant church (a catch-all sort of Protestant church). My earliest memory was the delight I felt while writing prayers to a God who was more a friend than an awesome authority to be feared. I would sneak into the Assembly of God summer-school sessions near my home without my parents' knowledge.

God was very real to these people, and they told me all I needed to do was to ask Jesus into my heart. I closed my eyes as hard as I could and from the earnest place from which only a child can appeal, asked God into my life.

But nothing changed. I wondered why God was not there for me. Was no one listening to my prayers? I wanted to be loved and cared for; there had to be more than I experienced in my home.

When I reached 13 and the age of confirmation, I pleaded with my parents to let me be confirmed with my cousins in the Lutheran church to which my grandmother belonged. The entire family moved over, and I started memorizing the Lutheran Doctrine.

During the summer after eighth grade, I worked for a Jewish family in Minneapolis as a mother's helper. It was my first real exposure to Jews. They did not seem very different from anyone else I knew, except some food was very different. I worked for this family for two summers.

I met my husband at age 17 and agreed to convert to Roman Catholicism upon our wedding day. I was not attached to being a Lutheran, and Catholicism had a mystique and a depth. I thought that Catholicism would be my religious home. I married the August after graduating from high school, and had our son, Joel, 14 months later. I had abandoned $5,000 in college scholarships in favor of a family and what I hoped would be love. But I married for all the wrong reasons, and I looked for God in all the wrong places.

I felt God for the first time when I had a Pentecostal "born-again" conversion experience. I spoke in tongues, and a joy surrounded me which I interpreted as God's presence. I attended five Bible study classes a week and prayer groups every other night. I eventually left the Pentecostal experience because it was too limiting, too judgmental for me. But the experience left me with a determination to still study religion.

I entered college when my daughter, Kim, entered kindergarten. A whole world opened before me. I studied world religions and found myself dancing from one tradition to the next in awe and wonder. I looked for ways for the world religions to talk to one another and wrote all my papers working toward this end. I became a vegetarian and meditated for two hours a day. My mind was clear. I felt creative and alive. I did not find a home in any of the traditions I studied, but I found certain elements with which I had an affinity. Buddhism became my specialty, and I plunged myself into it, trying to understand how Buddhists understood the world.

Yet all my studies left me, in the end, without a home. I could no longer be a Christian after studying Biblical texts. Jesus was a holy man to me: No longer God, he was a devout Jew. When I studied the Torah and the history of the Jewish people, my heart moved, yet I still did not have eyes to see a home. My soul cried out.

I moved to Japan, and before long, I left Catholicism, my family, and a total way of life. I was deeply alone. I moved back to California and felt a call to convert to Judaism. I had gone to several synagogue services with a Jewish friend in Japan, had been touched by my studies in the Torah, and was left empty by the other religions I had been studying. But with Judaism, a voice welled up in me: "You are home. You have finally come home." Tears welled up in my eyes. I had never had this reaction before with any religion I had studied or participated in.

What did it mean to be home? I found myself working through and becoming part of this religious tradition. I emotionally and spiritually went through a profound initiation. The Jewish community continued to ask, "*Why* are you doing this? Are you sure you want to do this?" It was a bewildering question. Yet, not once did I question that this was the step I wanted to take. I was scared, but prepared, thanks to my teacher who had lovingly nurtured me through the two-year process of personal and emotional change. When I stepped into the waters of the *mikveh* (ritual bath used in the conversion ceremony) and became a Jew, my soul felt at rest. There was peace, not thunder and lightning. My most moving experience in this process was when I stood before the ark and the congregation and publicly announced my decision to become a Jew. I had found Jerusalem, and now had to begin building my home.

I still do not always feel Jewish. Yet, I recently went to a synagogue and re-discovered that, yes, I am a Jew. I have the soul of a Jew. I just have to build my home in the city that is Jewish. Each year, I will add another room, a window, a door, a piece of furniture. At the end of my lifetime, God willing, I will have my Jewish home right in the middle of Jerusalem.

SOMETHING SHARED
by Shoshana

MY FAMILY IS CHINESE. I GREW UP IN TAIPEI, A
large, urban city on Taiwan. Both my mother and father came
from large families and moved to Taiwan from China, due to the
Chinese Civil War of the 1940s. They are not Buddhist, although
many Chinese are, and, in fact, they grew up with virtually no
religious affiliations. My mother's family was quite well off in
China, but became lower middle-class after moving to Taiwan.
My father was poor and escaped to Taiwan with no other family
members. Both my parents are very humble and have strong family values, which was very much a part of my upbringing.

I had no religious influences until my high school years,
when many of my friends at school were Christians. They often
asked me to join their Bible study classes and attend services. I
attended a few times, but became more negative about
Christianity as I did. I was not comfortable about all the attention
Christians gave to pleasing God and Jesus Christ so they would

Shoshana, a 35-year-old raised with no formal religion,
converted to Judaism eight years ago.

63

have a good afterlife. To me, it seemed like a "behave-this-way-or-burn-in-hell"-type religion.

I had little understanding of Judaism when I met Steven, my husband, who is an Iranian Jew. About a year later, when Steven and I started dating, my parents felt comfortable with this "racially mixed" situation. This was partially because they had known him for over a year and they liked him, and also because they knew that he was Jewish. My mother was impressed by the strong family values of her Jewish friends.

My conversion process began rather painfully and stressfully. Steven had not told me how "unpleased" his parents were with the idea that I was not Jewish. He had never really told me how important this was to them, and maybe he had not let himself be fully aware of it. We had long talks together. Once I realized the gravity of the situation, I told him I did not want him to marry me only if I converted. I wanted time to learn about the religion and to make this decision when I had enough knowledge to do so. I wanted him to be sure that he *did* want to marry me, and not have to regret this if I chose not to convert. We decided to meet with a rabbi to discuss the possibilities of conversion and marriage.

The first rabbi we met discouraged us from pursuing whatever plans we had. First, he said that he did not perform interfaith marriages, even though I had no formal religion. But he offered to give me lessons and outlined his conversion process. I had heard from friends that rabbis will ask you many questions—some negative—to make sure that you really want to convert. But I was not happy with his attitude. He came across as very negative and demeaning. Nor did I like how he was viewing our situation. For example, he had Sunday classes in Judaism for potential converts. In our area, it is customary for couples to attend the classes together (which Steven and I both wanted to do), but because we had jobs for which Sunday was the most important day, we could not attend them. When we told the rabbi this, he said that he felt we were not really serious about converting if we were not willing to commit ourselves to attending Sunday classes. I was very upset at how he came to this conclusion, even though we said we would be happy to make special trips anywhere in our area for classes during the rest of the week. It seemed like a very petty thing on which to base such a serious remark.

We then found a rabbi in nearby Seattle who had nighttime classes during the week. We met him, talked, and decided to attend his classes. We both attended these classes on a weekly basis for about three months, and he was happy to perform our wedding. After finishing these classes, we could think and talk about my conversion without linking it to any pressures of marriage or family. In time, we were introduced to the woman who would be my conversion tutor. By now, I was pregnant, and I hoped I could complete my conversion before having my baby.

The conversion process was pleasant and illuminating. I learned much about Judaism—and about my husband. Because he attended the classes with me, I had a chance to hear his opinion on many subjects we had never discussed before. I also found out how his family practiced religion, and I learned much about his values. But as I was learning about the practices of Judaism, I didn't see Steven doing many of them in his own daily life. I talked with the rabbi and Steven about this and came to understand that, just as with any religion or belief, there are many interpretations of the same thing. But basically, the most important values and ideas are shared and practiced.

My conversion process was very personal and organized. I really liked that. Although I had attended group classes, I felt that the most beneficial approach was my individual, private lessons with my teacher. Perhaps it was because I could study at my own pace, but also because I always felt my situation to be not quite the same as those of other interfaith couples because I had no prior religious affiliation. Thus, while there was not much to "unlearn," I did have to learn about the concept and belief in God.

My teacher and I developed a special relationship that I did not have with the rabbis. I was delighted to be invited to her home for the classes and for family dinners. I could freely discuss with her my pregnancy, my desire to raise my children in a Jewish environment, and my role as a mother and woman in such a household.

I initially shied away from the *mikveh* process, the ritual immersion for conversion, but I eventually realized that it was necessary to make my conversion complete. When I soaked in the waters of the *mikveh* with my eight-and-a-half month baby daughter inside my tummy, I felt proud that I had been able to complete my studies. It meant so much to me that she would be able to start her life with me as her Jewish mother.

Judaism now touches us every day. With the baby, it is possible to attend synagogue only irregularly, but my daughter attends nursery school at the local Jewish Community Center and I am very happy when I visit her class and see her learning prayers and songs. Recently, we visited my in-laws for the first time after our marriage. It was so nice to see how my conversion has pleased them and eased their concerns. My decision to convert to Judaism was one of the best and most important of my life. It has been a wonderful decision, not only for me, but for everyone in the family.

PERSONAL REDEMPTION
by Miriam

I WAS BORN IN WAR-TORN BERLIN. MY MOTHER WAS Protestant and my father was a *Mischling,* the name the Nazis gave to offspring between Jewish and non-Jewish parents. My father's father was of Orthodox Jewish descent. Because of that, he had not been able to marry my paternal grandmother since she was a Christian. My grandmother later married a Christian who adopted my father and gave him his name.

During the Hitler era, nobody could get married without proof of "Aryan" ancestry. My father would have been unable to produce such proof; even though he was raised as a Protestant he was considered "non-Aryan." No marriage took place between my parents and they broke up soon after my birth. My father later went to Venezuela for several years with his then-wife and their three children. My mother never married.

My paternal grandfather had immigrated in 1933 to Israel, which was then still Palestine. Many years later, I learned from my grandmother that he had married a non-Jewish woman before

Miriam, a 51-year-old former Protestant, converted to
Judaism seven years ago.

leaving Germany. My grandfather and his wife lived near Tel Aviv.

My mother was raised in a non-religious family. My maternal grandfather called himself a free-thinker. Since he refused to have any of his eight children baptized, my mother was brought up without any religious training. I believe that for the mere fact that *she* had not been baptized, she wanted me to be, and I was.

In Berlin, which is predominantly Protestant, everyone has religious training in public school followed by confirmation classes. When I was learning about the Bible, it really didn't mean anything to me. Nor did my confirmation. I couldn't understand why I should believe in Jesus Christ since he had been dead for almost 2,000 years. I was also glad I didn't have to go to services anymore, Sunday after Sunday.

Over the years, I became quite distant from any Christian doctrine and, deciding to follow in my maternal grandfather's footsteps, I called myself a free-thinker.

My father had returned from South America during the mid-1950s and was living in Cologne with his wife and children. He had become a Jehovah's Witness and tried to persuade me to join him. This incident was actually a turning point since I decided then I did not want to be Christian.

One of the things I had told my father when he wanted me to be a Jehovah's Witness was that if one really wants to choose a religion, the "right" one should be Judaism because that is where it all began. Even though I made this statement with deep conviction, I did not pursue Judaism at the time, probably, I think, because I did not know anything about it and was not very inclined to find out, mostly because of my youth.

I first heard about the Holocaust from a book my half-brother showed me, *The Yellow Star*. It shocked me tremendously. I grew up and went to school during the 1950s when history lessons did not mention the Holocaust and barely taught anything about Hitler and World War II. I was totally ignorant about any details of the war. At home, no one spoke of "Jews."

I never thought that I had Jewish ancestry. I was only glad to know that my family had not participated in the horrors of the Hitler era. My maternal grandfather was not only irreligious but also apolitical, and had refused to join any party during the Hitler regime. When I married in 1971 and came to the United States a year later, our lives were also very non-religious.

I eventually became an aide to a teacher in the ESL (English as a Second Language) program in the San Jose schools. The teacher was Jewish, and we became very good friends. She invited me to her house to celebrate Passover with her and her family. The experience changed my life. It was joyous and heartwarming and left me with the desire to finally learn more about Judaism.

Gradually, I started observing Jewish laws (under my friend's tutelage) and participated in a Learner's *Minyan* at her synagogue. I have been going to *shul* (synagogue) ever since. In the months since then, I started attending conversion classes. I haven't had any doubts that I am doing the right thing. I feel Jewish and I feel a strong bond with the Jewish people. This year, Passover meant a lot more than it did last year. I, too, had been delivered from bondage!

When I went to the memorial services last April for the victims of the Holocaust, I was very, very moved. I felt a pain, not only for the Jews lost during the Holocaust, but for the German nation as well. They had been my people and they had done this horror to the Jews, who were also my people. I cannot ever accept the atrocities of those Germans. Out of this contempt over their crimes came the hope that perhaps I can somehow redeem their actions by becoming a Jew. If one German becomes Jewish, maybe one of the six million Jews can be brought back to life.

I want to convert to Judaism for spiritual reasons, but also for emotional reasons. I have always looked for the purpose in things that happened and things that did not happen. I now believe that I was not destined for a non-Jewish life. By converting to

Judaism, I will find a true purpose in life.

Through my many trials and tribulations, I sometimes wondered if my long journey would ever end. I now realize that I, too, spent forty years in the desert and that I am finally going home to my people.

So where am I headed? As Johann Wolfgang von Goethe, the great German poet, writer and philosopher, once said, "Noble be man, helpful and good, for that distinguishes him from all things we know." I want to look back on my life and say that I was noble, helpful and good, for those are the qualities of a righteous Jew. And I really hope to attain inner peace, one that comes from the conviction that life has truly been fair. I have looked for resolutions all my life, for answers to my questions. The answers must lie with God—and they must be found with God's infinite wisdom.

STEP BY STEP

by Naomi Devorah

MY PATH TO JUDAISM HAS BEEN LONG AND WINDING.
Now twenty-seven, I am an attorney with a background in social
work. For as long as I can remember, I have been interested in
helping people, in goodness and in finding God. I am married to
a highly assimilated Jew whose own religious involvement was
first stirred ten years ago at an adult weekend at a Jewish camp.
Together, we have tiptoed toward Judaism for several years.

My life began in Guatemala, where I came from a relatively
wealthy family. As a child, I was raised as a Catholic and attended
religious instruction for several years. My mother left the church
upon her divorce. I was seven, which is when we fled to the
United States. Over the years, we joined—and left—several
Christian churches, as well as flirted with the occult. We were des-
perately poor, and my mother supported me and my younger
brother by cleaning houses and cooking for wealthy families. We
had little contact with Jews, so I only became aware of Judaism
when I was in junior high school. I grew up in an integrated

Naomi Devorah, a 29-year-old former Catholic, converted
to Judaism three years ago.

71

neighborhood and went to school with a wonderful mix of people: Jews, African-Americans, Hispanics, "WASPS" and Asians. Over time, most of my friends tended to be Jewish, and I started to respect (and envy) their lifestyle. All came from families with two parents who were very much involved in parenting, in loving their children, and in taking good care of them. My Jewish friends were confident about themselves and they believed in God, and I so much wanted to be part of a culture in which family life was important and where religion played such an integral role. My friends "adopted" me, and I was soon sharing their dreams: If they could be professionals, so could I. If they could get excellent grades, so could I. If they could embrace one God, so could I.

My relationships with Jews continued more or less the same way over the years, but my most important relationship has been with Albert, who I married two years ago. He is wonderful, caring, intelligent and patient. He was born in South Africa, and his family migrated to the United States when he was a toddler. His mother is from Lithuania; his father is from England. Members of his mother's extended family were killed in the Holocaust, and most of her immediate family lives in Israel.

I have learned a lot from Albert's mother. She has taught me about persecution against Jews throughout history, and shared with me many of her experiences as a Jew, both good and bad. She told me of being expelled from her German class in rural South Africa because of the dominant *Hitler Jugen* youth movement in her school. She taught me of the isolation she felt when her best friend told her they could no longer see each other. She told me of running away from home at 18 to join the South African army, and how she became a sergeant during the Second World War. Although she had had a very strict Orthodox upbringing, as an adult she became strongly opposed to any form of organized religion. While she certainly considered herself to be a Jew, she strenuously rejected Judaism. Sadly, Albert grew up in a household without *Shabbat* candles and without holiday observances.

My love for Judaism has awakened in Albert an interest in being Jewish. He and I have begun to have *Shabbat* dinners, attend *Shabbat* services when we can, and observe the major Jewish holidays. We belong to a *havurah* (Jewish fellowship group), and we've put a *mezuzah* (ritual object affixed to the doorway of Jewish homes) on our door. He and I have also committed ourselves to raising our children as Jews.

I choose Judaism for what it offers me: A tradition, a history, and a lifestyle which can guide me and my family through the years. One of Judaism's mysteries is how Jews have survived 4,000 years of persecution while contributing so much to society. The Einsteins, the Salks, the entertainers, the bankers, the lawyers, the philosophers have all contributed to what the world is today. Jesus, Marx and Freud are products of this remarkable people, as are others who help shape modern American society. Something in Judaism creates such people, and I want my family to share in that magic.

What has touched me most in my studies has been the Holocaust. For the first time in my life, I learned to face the hard truth about what happened under the Third Reich. To me, the Holocaust no longer means "Six Million Jews Died." It means that *my* people died because the whole world let it happen. I have a greater sense of appreciation for the Jews and a greater understanding about why the Jews are so concerned with maintaining their identity and their community: Often banned from fully participating in society, we were forbidden from owning land and holding office and were forced to live in ghettos. We endured pogroms and crusades. Our synagogues were destroyed. We were killed, forced to convert, and expelled from our land. I have also learned about the State of Israel. I must admit that I could never understand why people made such a big deal about such a little country, and why such a little country made so much noise.

Having now read and seen films about the helplessness of European Jews during the Holocaust, and now realizing the callousness of governments around the world that refused sanctuary to refugees before, during and even after the war, having read about pogroms and expulsions throughout the centuries, I now realize how naive I was. While I still take issue with some specific policies of Israel's government, the necessity of a Jewish state is beyond question.

Beyond Israel as a refuge, I also appreciate Israel as an opportunity. Never before have Jews had the opportunity to work together to build a society or to put our political, economic, artistic and scientific genius to work through the power of our own state. Israel is now a dynamic melting pot for Jews from around the world. Tormented with intractable difficulties, the country is also blessed with enthusiasm, dedication and inspiration. From such an environment, a great society is now maturing, and will for centuries be a light among nations.

The Jewish religion is very appealing to me. It is oriented toward creating better people: People who are good to one another, people who have respect and love for their environment. Judaism places the responsibility for one's life on one's self. It does not defer reward to an afterlife. It is a religion determined to create a just society of good people.

Judaism keeps one focused on the positive. It has a blessing for nearly everything: For bread, for *Shabbat* candles, for a newborn child, for the first fruit of the season. I have begun to appreciate the blessings such as the *Shehecheyanu*, the thanksgiving prayer, and have recited it upon seemingly insignificant moments in my life.

I have found attending services at our synagogue fulfilling and uplifting. My favorite services are those on Friday night. While I find the *Aleinu*, the closing prayer which speaks of the providence of God, the most inspiring of prayers, the one that touches me the most is the *Mourner's Kaddish*, the "mourner's prayer" which also praises God. Tears sometimes come to my eyes as I listen to the names of those who have died. It is so moving to think of their memory being carried with the congregation. As we all rise to pray for those who died in the Holocaust and who have no survivors to pray for them, I feel more tightly bound to the Jewish people and to our history.

I feel that I have been on the path to Judaism throughout my life. Actually declaring myself a Jew and being accepted as one by the Jewish community has been immensely meaningful to me. I feel that I have found a home.

CLAIMING MY JEWISH IDENTITY
by Elisheva Tzipora

IF YOU ASK A JEWISH PERSON WHY THEY HOLD SO dearly to their Jewish identity, the answers will vary. Some may cite tradition or wanting to honor their parents or to instill Jewish values in their children. They may cite Judaism's intellectual tradition. I, too, can come up with many reasons. Each is valid and meaningful. However, if I were challenged on each reason, I would have to offer the plain answer, "I can't explain it. I just want to be Jewish." When it comes down to it, I just know that I must be Jewish to feel complete with my past and to feel whole. This is something I can do only from within the Jewish community.

The point of all this is that there is a basic existential truth which cannot be rationally explained and which goes into the realm of intuition, personal truth and inner loyalty. Ultimately, it is like love: It just *is* and cannot be questioned beyond a certain point.

Elisheva Tzipora, a 32-year-old raised in Israel by a
Jewish father and a non-Jewish mother, converted to
Judaism two years ago.

I was born in Israel in 1959. My Jewish father was Polish-born and Israeli-raised. My mother was born and raised in Sweden as a Protestant. My father immigrated to Israel in 1935 at the age of two with his parents, his sister and his paternal grandparents. After a failed attempt at operating a dairy farm, my father's grandparents returned to Poland, where they died during the Holocaust. Both of my father's parents stayed in Israel until they died. My mother was introduced to Israel by my father after they were married in Rome. I think my mother was courageous to move from Sweden to Israel for no other reason than her love for my father. In addition, my mother never converted to Judaism, and she never quite integrated into Israeli society.

When my parents met, the question of my mother's conversion came up. My mother agreed to convert and began studying with a rabbi in Copenhagen. Toward the end of her studies, the rabbi recommended that she do the actual conversion ceremony in Israel, as she was going to live there. My mother agreed.

My parents were married before the end of her conversion. Since, this was technically an intermarriage, they could not be married in Israel. Instead, they had a civil wedding in Rome. Once they moved to Israel, my mother had to finish her conversion. Both my parents have never given me a straight answer to my questions about why she never finished her conversion. Instead, I hear blame on both sides. Neither assumes any responsibility for what did, or did not, happen.

As the first-born child, I believe that I absorbed the tensions between my parents regarding my mother's conversion. I was always ashamed of my mother for being different, and I never dared tell anyone except my closest friends that I was not Jewish.

A few years ago, while living in Paris, I began to desire more of a conscious Jewish life and realized how most of my Israeli friends in Paris, as well as my family in Israel, celebrated the major Jewish holidays by just going through the motions without experiencing any religious or spiritual pleasure. This quest eventually led to my conversion when I moved to California.

In spite of feeling a strong Jewish identity, it took living outside of Israel for a few years to be consciously aware of my religious and spiritual needs—and to take appropriate action to satisfy them. Maybe if I had stayed in Israel all my life, I would have never felt the need to affirm my Jewish identity. Growing up in a Jewish state gave me a Jewish identity which would have been harder to acquire if I had grown up elsewhere.

In other words, in Israel I was taught with a Jewish way of living on all levels. Even if I didn't go to synagogue every Friday or even if I didn't keep *Shabbat*, I was very aware of the significance of this day. In school every Friday, we lit *Shabbat* candles, sang songs and invited the *Shabbat* into our lives. All the Jewish holidays were celebrated at school and at home. As a result, in spite of not being "officially" Jewish, I grew up in a Jewish environment and with a strong Jewish identity.

Things changed once I left Israel and began wandering around Europe and the United States. Suddenly, I became aware of what I had taken for granted throughout my childhood. To feel Jewish now, I had to create an entire Jewish environment for myself. But even that was impossible since I was not living in a Jewish country. This realization, combined with meeting the man I would marry (who is also Israeli), coupled with a desire to move back to Israel and raise children in a Jewish environment, prompted me to convert.

I had always experienced my "unofficial" Jewish identity as a shameful punishment for something that I was not. And I always blamed my mother for not converting, and for making my life so complicated because she had not converted. However, part of the process of growing up has been realizing that no one was to blame. My father and my mother each made the best decisions they could at the time. I eventually saw conversion as a privilege unavailable to most Israelis: I could *choose* to become Jewish. It became obvious to me that, by converting, I could find aspects of

myself I had long lost. This was confirmed when I began studying with my tutor, who reintroduced me to Judaism in the best
possible way by spending many hours with me searching for the
roots and the meaning of biblical words, as well as discussing
Jewish values and customs.

I had originally planned to have an Orthodox conversion,
but I decided against it once I realized that I could not follow an
Orthodox way of life. I also feared that Orthodox Jews would not
accept me. In time, I learned about Reform Judaism, which I had
previously only heard about. Suddenly, everything fell into place.
I was introduced to a Judaism which did not unquestioningly
accept Torah as the word of God, but combined Jewish tradition,
philosophy and values with rational thought, believing in true
choice as part of living a Jewish life. I have found a way to integrate a Jewish way of living into my belief system without com-
promising my integrity.

I am now bathing in the bliss of having committed myself
to living a Jewish life and in the pride in my choice. I also plan
to continue searching for what I need from Judaism and what I
can offer it. I am especially interested in seeking the support of
women for my search for a Jewish identity that honors my wom-
anhood. I envision the rest of my life as an endless exploration
that will deepen my love for Judaism, as well as pass this love to
my children and to the community around me.

Each time I tell my mother about my desire to live a more
conscious, active Jewish life, she tells me about the first Passover
dinner in which I participated. I was four months old and spent
most of that *seder* in a crib by the dining room table. Present were
my mother, father, grandfather, aunt, uncle and my uncle's father.
Apparently, the two elderly men—my grandfather and my uncle's
father—spent the entire evening debating different ideas relating
to Passover. I want to believe that lying in the crib, silently listening to my elders' debate, I was impregnated with my first love for
Judaism, and that the rest of my life has been a search for the same

feeling that I had when I was four months old.

My son, whom I carry within me as I write these words, is due to be born four evenings before Passover. Knowing the unpredictability of due dates, especially with a first-born, I hope he will be born by Passover so that he can participate in his first *seder*. But if he should choose to stay within me for a few more days, I hope he will be filled with the essence and the spirit of this holiday as he listens silently to the words of all of us present at the *seder* table.

GLEANINGS

Long before I became a Jew, I attended a seder *at which a woman who was present told of her survival at Auschwitz. She had a profound effect upon me: I will never forget her.*

This was the seder *before I went to Eastern Europe, where I found myself in Prague. In a small museum, there were Torah mantles; pieces of wood and fabric from synagogues; old books and printing presses. And upstairs, there was artwork done by the children who perished in Terezin, the Nazi concentration camp in Czechoslovakia where 15,000 children perished between 1942 and 1944. Each picture was labeled with the child's name. I was there for hours, crying. It broke my heart.*

That night, after I wrote a brief summary of the day in my little notebook, I added this entry: "What a strong connection I feel to Judaism. I have to consider making my decision about conversion." It was the first time I had put my feelings into words.

My conversion took place two years later.

—P'NINA

For me, converting has been like returning to a home that I have vaguely pictured in my mind for many years. It's a home that feels comfortable and familiar, but which had several new rooms added while I was away on my spiritual journey. The rooms have names on them, such as "Israel," "Jewish educa-

tion" and "community service." My responsibility is to explore these rooms and incorporate what I find in them into my Jewish existence.

—RISHON MEIR

I look at the changes I made in my life and I see that I was right. I want to practice Judaism, and I have the same zeal I did when I started. I am now divorced from the Jewish man to whom I was married when I started taking lessons in Judaism. I have moved to a new town in a new state. I have lost touch with many of the friends I used to know. But I am still very much a Jew, and Judaism is more important to me every day. My recent move was eased because I could walk into a new synagogue and feel comfortable talking to strangers, because I could hang a mezuzah (ritual object affixed to the doorway of Jewish homes) on my door and say, "This is my home." —MICHAL

In my conversion studies, I've learned history, some Hebrew, Jewish ethics, holidays, the Jewish life cycle, Jewish law, Jewish customs, and much more. But my journey into Judaism has mostly been an emotional one: Learning what it feels like to walk into a synagogue and know that it is my place. Listening to the cantor's beautiful voice and letting it carry me away. Sitting at my friend's Passover seder table and listening to his eight-year-old son ask the Four Questions. Being in services and feeling excitement that I knew enough Hebrew to follow

along. Standing with my hands covering my eyes and reciting the blessing over the Shabbat *candles for the first time. Reading Leon Uris'* Exodus *and crying when the State of Israel was founded. Looking at my husband at* Shabbat *services as he sings the* Bar'khu *and thinking how beautiful he looks in a* kippah *(ritual headcovering).*
—MALKA ELISHEVA

My conversion marks a very important time for me: The beginning of sharing my values, feelings and self, rather than the formal completion of becoming a Jew.
—BARA

SECTION IV

Turning Faith into Action

Let Your tender mercies be stirred for the righteous, the pious, the leaders of the House of Israel, devoted scholars and faithful proselytes... Praised are You, Lord, who sustains the righteous.

—FROM THE DAILY AMIDAH
(the silent devotional prayer central to every Jewish service)

EMBRACING THE COVENANT

Conversion to Judaism is as much a *process* as it is a transformation. It has been said that the important element in becoming a Jew is contained in the labor which accompanies that choice.

This transformation is a natural, yet miraculous phenomenon, comparable to the emergence from the chrysalis of a butterfly that has not yet proved it can fly. Its first flutterings are hopeful and tentative; the desire (the soul, or *nefesh*) is there, but the wind (the spirit, or *ruach*) is needed to support the flight. What has taken months and, in many cases, years to develop, now requires sustenance in order to thrive.

The *process* of converting can be overwhelming. It is meant to be. Conversion is an unforgettable moment in one's life, the epitome of a significant life-passage. As one "butterfly" said of this moment, "It was, next to the birth of my daughter, the happiest moment in my life!" Another said, "When the Rabbi handed me the Torah, I felt joined in history to generations of Jews!"

But after this peak experience, the butterfly must test its wings. This is often not easy to do.

The months of study and experience culminate in an emotional rite of passage, and one must now fashion a Jewish life. Qualities associated with successful maturation in society are replicated in the growth of a new Jewish soul: A supportive environment, ample opportunity to validate one's identity, models to imitate, and a network of like-minded peers. *With* these, the conversion is a positive, self-sustaining experience. Without them, one's Jewish growth may be stymied and frustrated.

The new Jew may possess a lack of knowledge about which Jewish step to take next or may be shy about approaching the formal Jewish community for further guidance. Meanwhile, the Jewish community may not extend a welcome to the "newly-Jewish." This may occur for fear of embarrassing them or an inability to effectively integrate them into synagogue life or a mutual lack of understanding of the high cost of Jewish living (synagogue dues, UJA pledge, summer camp, religious school, etc.). Some born-Jews may feel uneasy about the zeal exhibited by some Jews-by-Choice. If the convert is married to a born-Jew, the Jewish partner may be uncomfortable with the convert's strong desires to incorporate Judaism into their lives, desires which may have been previously absent from their relationship.

There is an important role for the Jewish community to play since, ideally, the Jew-by-Choice is surrounded by supportive, sensitive people. These may include extended family-members who will welcome the convert in religious celebrations and encourage participation on many levels. A non-judgmental, inclusive attitude helps immeasurably in fostering an active Jewish life in the convert. Most importantly, if the significant people in one's life are open and helpful to the Jew-by-Choice, the willingness to "try one's wings" is made easier, for as Rabbi Abraham Joshua Heschel said, being Jewish requires "a leap of action, rather than a leap of faith." It is in the *living* that we find the *being*.

One benefit of all of this to born-Jews is that through their relationships with Jews-by-Choice, *their* own Jewish identities will strengthen and sweeten as *they* vicariously experience Judaism through new eyes.

The following accounts tell of the tensions and challenges new converts faced, how they confronted them, and how their experiences gave them the wings to fully enter the mainstream of Jewish life.

GLEANINGS

The mikveh *(ritual bath used in the conversion ceremony) was nice. I emerged, not only a Jew, but as the mother in a Jewish household, a whole Jewish household. I felt that I had done something very important for my children, since they, too, became Jews along with me, as they converted at the same time I did.* —Sarah

The more I study about Judaism and the more I want to attend services, the less my family wants to join me. The kids are now teenagers with too many plans for Friday nights and have not absorbed enough tradition for it to make a difference to them. My husband has no desire to practice his Judaism or to attend services. He will occasionally join me if I make an issue out of it, but he never does so spontaneously or with enthusiasm. He seems to enjoy himself when he goes, but not enough to find that he has a desire to go again. If I pressure him into going, I feel guilty. If he doesn't go, I feel angry, alone, abandoned. My desire to be more involved with Judaism seems to make him uncomfortable. Instead of bringing us closer, Judaism seems to be pulling us apart. I have tried to deal with this problem in several ways, but sadly, we have not yet

found a comfortable solution: The more Judaism I bring into my life, the more I shut my Jewish husband out.
—SOER

The conversion process is laborious and long. That's good. It gives you a chance to truly know what you're getting into.
—LEBA ZAHAVA

A RETURNING

by Elisheva

ALTHOUGH THIS STORY REALLY BEGINS MUCH EARLIER, I'm going to begin it on a fall day in 1987. In one of those brief, illuminating moments which stay with one always, all was ripe for discovering my Jewish identity.

I arrived at that day having already experienced Jewish rituals and having learned in faint, undefined ways a little of what being Jewish meant. But I had still not connected these experiences to my identity. During my childhood, I had learned that my family had some connection to Judaism, but I had no idea what that meant. My mother had warned me that I was Jewish enough to have gone to the gas chambers and that, if any one in authority asked whether I was Jewish, I should answer no. Yet, I was taught the *Hamotzi* (blessing over bread) and I ate Jewish food. Still, I didn't understand how all this affected me or made me Jewish.

When I was seven, my grandparents were over for dinner and I was asked to bless the food. Naturally, I decided to say my

Elisheva, a 28-year-old with a Jewish father and Catholic mother, converted to Judaism seven years ago.

favorite blessing. As I began *"Baruch atta Adonai,"* I received a kick under the table. After dinner, I learned that I wasn't supposed to say the Hebrew blessings in front of my Catholic grandparents. All this greatly confused me.

"Why not?" I asked. "What is Hebrew? Does that mean I'm Jewish?"

I had so many questions which were unanswered. When I asked my Mom if I was Jewish or Catholic or what, she answered that neither she nor my father believed in religion and someday, when I was older, I would decide for myself.

But on this day in 1987, after eighteen years of learning, of discovering, of longing for something richer with which to identify, I began reading Abba Eban and Anne Frank. In college, I became fascinated with anything Jewish and settled on majoring in Judaic Studies. I had also begun to question some of the things I had been socialized into believing, such as being Jewish enough to be killed as a Jew, but not Jewish enough to be accepted by other Jews.

So on that day, which I chose to call the beginning of my Jewish existence, while reading from a book about the *Shoah* (the Holocaust), I suddenly saw myself sitting in a college library in one of the richest countries in the world. I had never known hunger, want, anti-Semitism, terrorism, torture or constant fear, yet I was reading about men, women and children who had been murdered for nothing more than having been born Jewish. And I cried there in the library. I cried of grief and shame and mourning. I felt the presence of these people and decided I would do whatever I could to strengthen *Am Yisrael* (the Jewish People). I turned forever away from my confusion and actively began leading a Jewish life.

I don't feel as did the biblical Ruth upon leaving her people and taking on another religious affiliation. For throughout my life, I have felt some cultural or ethnic bond to the Jewish people. Today, this bond is deeply rooted within my soul. Becoming

Jewish for me is *teshuvah*, a returning to part of my ancestry which had been denied me.

For three years now, I have lived my life as a Jew. I observe all the holidays. I keep kosher. I have even begun to celebrate some of the more obscure holidays, such as *Rosh Chodesh*, the minor festival celebrating the new month. Keeping the *mitzvot* (commandments) and standing for such Jewish values as giving *tzedakah* (charity), respecting your fellow human beings, opening your house to the less fortunate, and serving as prayer leader in synagogue, are the kinds of activities that I have been striving to make part of my life. Being a Jew means for me to recognize my faults and strive to overcome them. It means to always do better.

JUDAISM CHOSE ME!

by Rina

JEW-BY-CHOICE IS A SOMEWHAT ILL-FITTING TERM.
Yes, in a literal sense, I *chose* to be Jewish. I was raised
Episcopalian, married a Jew, and several years later went through
the conversion process and became Jewish. It was something I
wanted very much to do, with no particular pressure from anyone else to do so.

Yet, in some very real sense I didn't so much choose Judaism
as Judaism chose me. I never had felt totally comfortable as a
Christian. Even as a child, I sensed I was out-of-sync with some
Christian beliefs and practices. When, subsequent to my marriage,
I first attended *Shabbat* services, I quickly felt at home. My values,
ethics, sense of fairness were all reflected in Jewish tradition.

When I decided several years after that first synagogue visit
to declare to the world what it seemed my heart had always
known, I wanted more than anything else to enhance my sense
of belonging. My heart already belonged to Jewish theology; I
now wanted to belong to the Jewish people. Today, three years

Rina, a 36-year-old former Episcopalian, converted to
Judaism three years ago.

96

after my conversion, my quest is not complete: A true sense of belonging continues to elude me.

Jewish tradition teaches us that, once we become Jewish, we are no different from any other Jew. We need never speak of our non-Jewish past or of our conversion status. I have found that this is not so easy to put into practice. To ignore or deny my non-Jewish past is to forget about 33 years of my life. To only speak of the secular holidays of my past requires carefully editing my background and avoiding questions which might put my religious background into the conversation. In some ways, it is to also disavow my parents' identity and contributions to my life, though they loved me after my conversion as they loved me before.

Acknowledging these realities has made me become what I never wanted to be: A sort of ambassador for conversion. When friends know of someone who is considering conversion, they ask me for advice. I listen with empathy to their situation, even while I am saddened by this distinction between myself and other Jews.

Not all of my feelings of alienation relate to being a Jew-by-Choice. During the first *Rosh Hashanah* after my conversion, I resolved to become more involved in my synagogue. Unfortunately, a short time after the High Holy Days, the congregation was ripped apart by a bitter political struggle. Dues were increased without explanation or regard to one's financial circumstances; staff was hired and fired according to the whims of a select few. I remained there for two more years, but eventually realized the hurt was too deep: It made little sense to belong to such an institution.

Also, the past four years have been difficult for me personally. I have endured a chronic, painful depression while struggling to sustain a troubled marriage. The career which I had hoped would bring me some financial independence has yet to bear fruit; and I have watched, heartsick, while my teenager continued his self-destructive behavior. I have needed the love and support of my Jewish community. I have yet to find it.

I recently heard two stories of Jews-by-Choice who walked away from their newly-found faith. Being Jewish wasn't working out for them, and each declared that they were no longer a Jew. This image of Jews shedding their religion like an outmoded article of clothing frightens me. I wonder how much their not belonging to the Jewish community played a role in their decision to "quit." One woman angrily told me that she had tried her best for ten years to be a fully participating community member. Since she was never fully accepted, she would just as soon not bother trying anymore.

As for myself, I continue to try to find my place within the community. I recently joined a small congregation which is just starting. I am excited by the chance to help something wonderful grow from the hopes and dreams of a group of committed Jews, and I am cautiously optimistic that I can become an integral part of the congregation.

Not all of my lack of connection with the Jewish community relates to my being a Jew-by-Choice. Some is about the Jewish community being fragmented and tenuous in a predominantly Christian environment. Some has to do with my own individual psyche and wounds. I think, though, that perhaps Jews-by-Choice are particularly vulnerable to a lack of community connection. Maybe, like myself, many Jews-by-Choice rely on a congregation as their only Jewish family, having been rejected by their Jewish in-laws, either before, or even after converting. In some ways, a Jew-by-Choice is not unlike a Jewish child who needs nurturing and support. Outreach programs for post-conversion Jews need to be expanded. To be successful, they must rely on Jews of all backgrounds, not just Jews-by-Choice. Most of all, we need to remember that conversion is not so much an end as it is a beginning.

THE LONE SURVIVOR

by Miriam Hannah

MY EARLIEST RECOLLECTION OF MY RELIGIOUS HISTORY occurred on Hanukkah in 1965. I was five years old. The cantor in synagogue handed me a fifty-cent piece, and I never forgot how kind he was. In fact, all my memories of my childhood religious celebrations center around Hanukkah when my father, my sister and I would all be together and light the candles, play games, open gifts and finally eat *latkes* (potato pancakes).

My father is Jewish. My mother is not. When they divorced, I was raised by my mother. Although I considered myself a Jew, *halakhah* (Jewish law) stipulated that I was a gentile because Jewish lineage is transmitted by the mother. (The Reform and Reconstructionist movements now hold that Jewish lineage is passed through the father, as well as the mother.) This caused much heartache for me.

After I married and had two daughters, it meant a lot to me to officially become Jewish. I went through a conversion, not really to change my life, since I already considered myself Jewish, but to give this identity a formality that I and others could see. I

Miriam Hannah, a 35-year-old with a Jewish father and
a non-Jewish mother, converted to Judaism seven years ago.

really wanted my children to have a Jewish education and to enjoy the Jewish celebrations which I had cherished. Most of my feelings toward this decision were born of anger: I just couldn't believe that I wasn't considered Jewish when I had been living my life as a Jew—and I wanted to spare my children this pain.

But the conversion process greatly enhanced my self-esteem and clarified what I really wanted out of being Jewish. I learned a great deal, especially about Jewish history. This helped me know where I was coming from.

I didn't understand much of my own family's genealogy until I began these studies. I realized why, in the 1940s, letters stopped coming from family members still in Russia. Most were sent to concentration camps during the war. My father told me about relatives who had left the family because they were afraid to be Jewish when they came to this country.

When I told parents and siblings that I was pursuing a formal conversion to Judaism, they seemed confused. "Convert to what?" They didn't realize that most of our family *weren't* Jews. They had always assumed that if either of your parents were Jewish, so were you.

The people who were most proud of my decision were my father and his Aunt Tilly, one of the sisters in my father's family. She is especially proud of me because it turns out that I'm the first person in my family to do anything Jewish in over eighty years! There have been no *b'nai mitzvah* (ceremonies marking adolescents' entry into Jewish religious adulthood and responsibility) or Jewish weddings or *anything* Jewish in more than three-quarters of a century.

Because of my formal conversion, the Jewish link in our family isn't being lost. I see myself as a lone survivor, rather like a recessive trait in the sea of dominant traits of the genetic pool.

To my family, being Jewish was a curse. I believe that it depends on me to continue the faith, the culture, and the continued existence of our link to the Jewish people.

HOMEWARD BOUND: A
RETURN TO SINAI
by Michael

MY PARENTS WERE AGNOSTIC. FATHER BELIEVED IN the savior, Franklin D. Roosevelt. Mother favored nihilism and believed in the quiet, silent, finality of the grave.

The home was secular. We had a Christmas tree in December, but I was surprised to learn that some people had a religious belief around that tree and those presents.

When I was about ten years old, my mother announced that the next morning, Sunday, I would get up, put on nice clothes, and go to Sunday School with a neighboring family. I did as I was told. It was my first visit to a church. The small billboard in front advertised it as a Lutheran church. It was filled with people, some of whom I knew from school. Everybody sang and a man who dressed differently from the rest and was in charge of things gave a lecture based upon some text that I did not know.

I got home and waited for my mother to awaken. As she made her coffee, she asked me how it went. I told her and vol-

Michael, a 53-year-old raised with no formal religion, con-
verted to Judaism three years ago.

unteered that I was glad I did not have to do that again. "Yes," she said. "You do. You have to go every Sunday."

Every Sunday I did go, and every Saturday night I told my mother that I did not want to go to Sunday School. She would ask why. Because, I told her, I wanted to sleep late or because there was a neat movie on TV or because I was bored in Sunday School or because of any one of a hundred reasons. All to no avail. I was told I had to go.

One Saturday was different. This time when my mother asked why, I gave her what was probably a very poorly framed and fledgling theological argument. I do not remember the particulars, but the flavors are with me still. I explained how love and peace were preached week after week. Yet, the previous week, an intolerant statement had been made about Roman Catholics by the man in charge of this church. My mother smirked and said I did not have to go to Sunday School ever again. I had learned the lesson she wanted taught.

Then I went to junior high school, which was sheer terror. I made a few friends, most of whom were big guys or tough guys because that offered me protection. And then there was Amanda. One day in class, Amanda reached down to pick up something and a Star of David on a necklace tumbled out from her blouse. I asked her if that meant that she was Jewish. Yes, she was. We then had lots to talk about that was much more interesting than Archie and Jughead or even the vocabulary list. I do not remember specifics, but she worked real hard on getting me to make the right sounds as I sang "*Hava Nagila.*"

I missed Amanda when she moved away.

High school was better. I had friends like Tom and Harry, but I also had Jewish friends like Mark, Jamie and Rosie.

At some point in high school, I began to read about Judaism. I remember how comfortable I was with what I read.

My buddy, Mark Schwartz, was the first person to ask me if I were Jewish. I do not know why he asked.

Jamie used to invite me to spend the night. His mom lit candles on Friday evening, but I remember no other signs of religious observance. Jamie's dad surprised me with a statement about the Russians, whom we were all taught to hate in those Cold War days. He said that he did not hate the Russians because they killed a lot of Germans and every dead German was one less who could attempt to murder him.

A new neighbor moved into the house next door. He had a boiler repair business. He put in a pool, and I became friends with one of his sons, David. I spent most of my non-school hours in that pool or learning to play eight-ball on their pool table.

One day, there was a problem with the pool plumbing. Mr. Kavanaugh sent one of his workers to the house to fix the mechanism. I saw the look in the man's eyes. I saw the serial number tattooed on his forearm.

After high school graduation, I volunteered for the draft. After training, I was sent to an underground communication site seventy miles from Washington, D.C. I was inside a mountain site in 1967 when the Six-Day War started. The colonels, the majors, the senior sergeants and all the rest of us thought it was all over. We buttoned up tight, as America's military prepared for a nuclear exchange. My opinion that America should risk the nation in order to guarantee the survival of Israel was a minority opinion in my peer group.

Vietnam, 1968; The Mekong Delta. I acquired an understanding about the preciousness of life. I saw life taken, and I saw life given up willingly.

I had close calls. We all did. I was in a temporary wooden bunker one night during the Tet Offensive. There was some shooting, nothing bad. A loud thump rocked me back from my firing position. The next morning, I discovered a rifle-propelled grenade that had hit the bunker in front of where I stood, and had not exploded. My life was spared.

This incident raised a question common to all survivors:

Why me? It made me realize that I believed in God, that I loved God, that I was angry at God. I also realized that I did not believe in organized religion, which at that time I equated with Christianity.

Much later, I met a woman who belonged to a Jewish congregation in our area. She referred me to an Introduction to Judaism class at her synagogue. I learned basic things and saw how to progress on my own. I met some wonderful people who were returning to religious observance and others who were converting for one reason or another.

The class was an adventure, or perhaps more accurately, the "trailer" for an adventure yet to come.

The teacher invited me to her *seder* (the evening meal and ritual with which Passover begins) on the second night of Passover. It was one of the most memorable nights of my life.

Somewhere along the way, I made an emotional commitment to Judaism. Prior to that, my commitment, if that is the right word, was primarily intellectual. Soon came a spiritual awakening and a different way to relate to my fellow humans.

Now I know that Judaism has given me something powerful: A voice. I found it while going through this process of conversion. I use it now.

When I began my conversion, the rabbi with whom I was studying asked if I was converting in order to marry a Jew. I told him, "No." He asked a few more times as I worked with him. At first, I was unable to clearly explain to the rabbi that I was converting because of the emotional and spiritual connection I felt toward Judaism. Today, I can find the words to describe that special connection I, as a Jew, have with God. I know the Covenant, I know the responsibilities, and I know the rewards.

Last year, as my business took me all over the United States, I experienced many Jewish communities. I met Jews in Atlanta, in Portland, Anchorage, Stamford, Orlando, San Diego. I even met some Satmar Hasidim who were shopping in Middletown, New

York. The diversity and the uniformity made each experience exciting, unique—and comfortable. All these Jews share Sinai with me. In our hearts is "*Sh'ma Yisrael, Adonai Eloheinu, Adonai Echad*"— "Hear, O Israel, the Lord is our God, the Lord is One."

I have found freedom in the disciplines my people have accepted for generations. The *mezuzah* (ritual object affixed to the doorway of Jewish homes) on my front door does remind me, as I come and as I go, to be true to who I am and how I have chosen to live with others and with myself. On the wall behind my desk hangs a large piece of art with the stylized Hebrew words, "*Tzedek! Tzedek, tirdof,*" "Justice! Justice, you shall pursue!"

I am now *shomer kashrut* (observant of the kosher dietary laws). But keeping kosher can be troublesome. While all my non-Jewish friends and business associates accept my special dietary requirements, some Jews do not. I have been told, "Well, there is more to being Jewish than not eating pork...." (My response of "...and less, too," has fallen on deaf ears.) One Jewish woman even referred to my dietary observance as "an eating disorder."

I recently went to Israel with a Jewish singles group from the San Francisco Bay Area. The trip was led by the rabbi of my congregation. Landing in Tel Aviv, we got onto the bus which took us right to the *Kotel,* the Western Wall. The twenty minutes I spent at the Wall were the most moving and therapeutic of my life: I prayed and I cried.

There are some very hard things for me to deal with now. I struggle with Hebrew, which I feel I need to learn to read so I can acquire knowledge without the help of another person.

But that isn't the hard part. The hard part isn't talked about much. I am accepted by my congregation and by most of my new Jewish family. I am certainly accepted as a Jew by every anti-Semite. But how unusual that not every Jew includes me in his or her concept of *Klal Yisrael,* the unity of the Jewish people. Orthodox Jews do not accept me because my conversion was not done by an Orthodox rabbi. I have been told "It is the problem of the Orthodox," by people who had the good sense to choose Jewish mothers. But it is my problem, too. Were I to make *aliyah*, immigrate to Israel, I couldn't marry there. And because no Orthodox rabbi would bury me there, what would happen to my body when I died in Israel? Would I, as one who is not recognized by Israel as being Jewish, be denied burial in a Jewish cemetery?

The rich texture of my life as a member of the Jewish community will never become routine because I was almost fifty years old before becoming a part of it. There's the thrill of seeing my letter published in the regional Jewish newspaper, the joy of having a friend call me on my car phone to ask "the mobile *Mashgiach*" (the *kashrut* "expert") a question that I could answer; the honor of being asked to help someone make her kitchen kosher; the pleasure of financially contributing to a community driven by the concept of *tikkun olam*, making the world a better place. There is all this, and more.

I do not know where I will end up. Given the warmth and the family feeling of the Friday evening services and the pleasure of studying Torah, I know these are in my life to stay.

I am very much aware that I am on a journey without a destination. I have such a rich auger in Judaism that I expect to grow beyond my current comprehension of what is possible or obtainable.

Conversion provides me with an authentication. Rabbis decided that I know enough, that I understand enough, that I feel enough to be allowed to cast my lot with the Jewish people. My only regret is that I did not begin this life years ago.

A JOURNEY HOME
by Daniel

"I'VE READ THAT THE TORAH REMINDS AND DIRECTS the Jewish people thirty-six times to welcome the stranger. I was a stranger who never felt more welcome than when I met you. Thank you for being here as I become a 'Jew-by-Choice.' I contend, however, that everyone here today is a 'Jew-by-Choice.' Your willingness to live life Jewishly means that you've chosen to be Jewish. So, I now join you, the self-chosen."

So I spoke at my conversion ceremony. Growing up as a Catholic in the 1950s on the East Coast, I had been taught that the Jews had killed Christ and were therefore, somehow, responsible for all the ills of life. But in eighth grade, I saw a film on the Holocaust that was subsequently banned from viewing by the Catholic Church. I can remember to this day, forty years later, where I was standing in the hallway of my school as I came out of the darkened class after watching that film. I knew in my heart that what I'd been told about the Jews was wrong. In high school, I read a book, *Silent Is the Vistula*, about the uprising in Warsaw,

Daniel, a 50-year-old former Roman Catholic, converted
to Judaism two years ago.

107

and saw Jews for the first time not as stereotypes, but as humans. God for me was God the Father, a saintly old man in long white robes. God was also the Son he'd sent to earth. In college, I fell away from the faith of my youth, but remained convinced that there was a God who knew and loved me. Twenty years later, I wondered what had become of my close tie to the God of my youth.

At that time, Jews began to come into my life. I found myself meeting and working with Jews, serving on boards and committees with Jews, dating Jews, being befriended by Jews. This "coincidence" (a coincidence is described as a miracle in which God chooses to remain anonymous), coming at the same time as I was struggling to reunite myself with God, caused me to return to the Catholic Church.

But I quickly realized that the Hebrew Bible would be all that I needed to complete my return to God. I came to believe that I was truly Jewish, but had somehow been born into a Christian family.

In my excitement over recognizing this coincidence, I immediately rushed to devour all that I could on everything Jewish. Since all of my Jewish acquaintances were Reform Jews, I gravitated toward their congregation. I took an "Introduction to Judaism" course, read dozens of books, subscribed to the *Jerusalem Post*, talked about God and Jews until my friends decided that I would soon enroll in the rabbinate.

Never, however, did anyone encourage me to convert. Puzzled by this, I started to broach the topic. The response was always the same, "Why would you want to convert?" I knew that the *Noachide* laws required that non-Jews follow only seven commandments, but I was certain that wasn't the reason for my friends' reticence. One day, I read an article that identified their attitude's psychological underpinnings: "Why would a sane person choose to join a historically persecuted minority?" I knew immediately that until I could answer that question, I could not move any further toward Judaism.

Fortunately, God knows my heart and spoke to it. After about a year, I realized that the problem with the question was how it was phrased. Essentially, it was impossible to answer, rather like Catch-22. It was simply a modern cloaking of the Jewish tradition that a proselyte be asked three times to announce their intention to convert. One Saturday in synagogue, I recited the prayer thanking God for making me a Jew. I felt that the words were true for me. I was home.

After three years of study and prayer, I completed my conversion. I was ritually circumcised, immersed in the *mikveh* (ritual bath used in the conversion ceremony) and announced to friends and family that I would live as a Jew. Soon, I completed a course of study with a terrific mentor, learned a modicum of prayerbook Hebrew, and was called to the Torah as a *bar mitzvah*. Later that year, I went to Israel to honor the age-old yearning to be in Jerusalem.

Now, I am at peace. I try to practice a simple form of *kashrut*, or keeping kosher. For me, *kashrut* is a form of prayer. It is my way to remind myself every day that I am a Jew. Whether I've always been a Jew is problematic. It is, in fact, not important since today, and every day, I am a Jew.

GLEANINGS

Over the last several months, I have begun to identify with the Jewish people. At some point, I don't know when, I began referring to the Jewish community and the Jewish people as "we," not as "they." There has also been a gradual change in my behavior and attitudes. I give more to charity. I am less likely to gossip at work. I telephone my grandmothers and brothers more often. I have a new appreciation for things I frequently took for granted in the past. I am also able to more and more identify myself as Jewish without being afraid of being thought an imposter. I look forward to more fully participating in the Jewish community and giving more of myself. This change, achieved in minute steps, reinforces for me that my conversion is not an end, but a beginning. I anticipate that it will be a lifelong process, one which I am eager to begin now that the emotional and psychological hurdle of conversion is past.

—DAPHNA

I wonder whether I am truly accepted by other Jews and whether I really understood what I have chosen. I continue to be drawn to the notion that Judaism makes everything holy, that it connects me to history and with the spirit of God. I don't understand why Jews who criticize Israel are so viciously attacked. I don't understand why the Jewish community doesn't reach out more effectively to the intermarried and to singles and gays. I don't understand why Judaism doesn't seek more converts. I continue to be troubled about why some Jews get so caught up with the recitation of their prayers that they neglect to think about the nature of God. It also bothers me that I am sometimes singled out by other Jews because I "don't look Jewish," whatever that means.

—NATAN

An important step towards expressing my identity as a Jew was accepting a power greater than myself. My willingness to choose God and live by God's set of rules, or mitzvot, *has given new strength and hope to me and my family. Though there is much more for me to learn and become, I now stand poised and ready for the next step in the process of becoming a Jew. I hope I am worthy of the task.*

—DAVID

AFTERWORD:
THE MEANING OF
CONVERSION

THE MEANING OF CONVERSION

The moment of conversion is truly awesome, perhaps as awesome in its own way as when the Patriarch Abraham answered the same call 4,000 years ago in a place called Ur of the Chaldees. Abraham harkened to a Voice which commanded him to leave his home, his family, and his prior way of life.

Rabbinic commentaries on the Torah on Abraham's spiritual journey tell us this indicates that even 4,000 years ago, Jews-by-Choice came to Judaism for compelling personal motives. In a real sense, Judaism is as much a religion of converts as it is a religion of birth. The *ger tzedek*, the "righteous stranger," is not born under the yoke of Torah nor "chosen" through birth. Indeed, Jewish tradition says that the soul of the *ger tzedek* is higher than that of the born-Jew. According to some rabbis, the decision to

choose is greater than the involuntary circumstance of Jewish bio-
logical birth.

At first, it might seem that the Jew-by-Choice experiences
the Voice differently than the Jew-by-Birth. The *Midrash*, the collection of rabbinic interpretations of Biblical passages, tells us that
at the moment the Torah was given at Sinai, the mountain was
lifted up and the heavens parted. There was lightning, thunder and
the sound of the *shofar* (the ram's horn). Under these circumstances, the Jews accepted God's Law. But for the *ger tzedek*, there
is no lightning, no thunder. For today's convert to Judaism, the
Voice speaks from within as it did 4,000 years ago to Abraham.

THE COVENANTAL EMBRACE

About one out of every thirty-five Jews in America is a Jew-by-
Choice. While they have come to Sinai by many different paths,
their destiny is now linked with that of the Jewish people. The
entire Jewish family is forever changed by the presence of this
"stranger in our midst." Both, in fact, are enriched by the presence of the other. The impulse to become a Jew is often beyond
reason. People may attribute their conversion to childhood experiences, family friends, falling in love, being drawn to ethical pre-
cepts. But there is more. Since the heart and the soul have their
own reasons, the Voice murmurs from within. It resonates like the
shofar heard long ago at Mt. Sinai. In fact, the Voice within *is* the
shofar at Sinai. In the end, the Jew-by-Choice and the Jew-by-
Birth stand together at Sinai, both hearing the *shofar* as it proclaims, "*Tekiah*, Embrace the Covenant!"

APPENDIX A:
THE PROCESS OF CONVERSION

Conversion is long and demanding. The lengthy process usually unfolds in this manner:

- Upon recognizing the desire to formalize a conversion, an individual may contact a rabbi. In Judaism, a rabbi is not an intermediary between God and humankind. Rather, the rabbi is a teacher who transmits Jewish tradition and values, and who sets the standards which must be embraced by those seeking to convert. The rabbi may, as in times past, dissuade the candidate to test his or her commitment. (The tradition, according to the great twelfth century sage, Maimonides, is to "draw close with the right hand, and to discourage with the left.")

- If the person is still interested in pursuing this path, the rabbi may recommend weekly classes, either in a group or on an individual basis. These may last several months or longer.

These classes consist of intensive discussion, probing, reading. Sometimes, students may read as many as fifty books or more. In conjunction with learning about Jewish history, customs, traditions and ceremonies and reading about the *mitzvot* (the 613 commandments in the Torah), some time is ordinarily devoted to studying the Hebrew language.

• Students attend worship services and congregational programs and gradually incorporate Judaism into their daily lives. Concurrent with all this, candidates meet regularly with their host rabbi, who monitors and encourages their spiritual development.

• At the conclusion of this process, the candidate for conversion may write a spiritual autobiography and even take a written test.

In the Orthodox and Conservative movements, the candidate meets with a *bet din*, a "court" of three rabbis. The *bet din* affirms the candidate's readiness and "authorizes" the actual conversion. Following this, the candidate is immersed in the *mikveh*, a ritual pool of water. By completely submersing oneself in the water and then reciting the appropriate liturgy, the *mikveh* immersion symbolizes the spiritual transformation of the soul. For male candidates, entrance into the covenant of Abraham includes circumcision. For those already circumcised, the ritual of *hatafat dam brit,* the taking of a tiny drop of blood from the penis, is performed as a symbolic circumcision.

Standards within the Reform and Reconstructionist movements vary from one congregation to the next. The Reform and Reconstructionist movements require that candidates for conversion declare acceptance of the Jewish faith and people before three adult witnesses, at least one of whom must be a rabbi. Although these movements have not, in the past, required that candidates for conversion undergo *hatafat dam brit*, this ritual may be required by individual Reform and Reconstructionist rabbis, and increasingly more rabbis are doing so. The Reconstructionist movement requires that the candidate for conversion be immersed in a *mikveh*, while the Reform movement does not set this as a requirement. Immersion in *mikveh* and *hatafat dam brit*, when not required by the sponsoring rabbi, may be chosen by the convert to further ritualize his/her conversion experience.

At conversion, a Hebrew name is bestowed upon the candidate to symbolize one's new identity. There is often a ceremony of welcome in the sanctuary before the open Ark. The newly-converted Jew is handed the Torah and then recites a pledge of loyalty to Judaism. This includes the *Sh'ma Yisrael*, the statement of God's unity. The rabbi may also recite the three-fold priestly benediction—a traditional blessing for the well-being of the Jewish people.

The pledge of loyalty recited by the candidate usually reads as follows:

> "Of my own free will, I choose to enter the eternal Covenant between God and the people of Israel and to become a Jew. I accept Judaism to the exclusion of all other religious faiths and practices. Under all circumstances, I will be loyal to the Jewish people and to Judaism. I promise to establish a Jewish home and to participate actively in the life of the synagogue and of the Jewish community. I commit myself to the pursuit of Torah and Jewish knowledge. If I should be blessed with children, I promise to raise them as Jews."

APPENDIX B
HOW TO BEGIN –
PRACTICAL ADVICE

"All beginnings are difficult," the *Midrash* reminds us. If anything is clear from our work with Jews-by-Choice over the years, it is that the act of conversion to Judaism *is* merely a beginning. It is far from the "end" of Jewish identification. Rather, it is the beginning of integration into the Jewish community. As an old "*bubbe-meisa*," a folk saying, puts it: "After the wedding, there is the marriage."

For those of you who are considering whether Judaism is for you, here is some advice from those who have already converted:

Meet with several rabbis to learn more about the conversion process.

Every rabbi approaches conversion a little differently. Some are fairly structured; others are less rigid. Choose one with whom you are most compatible. Explore a broad spectrum of rabbis among the various movements to determine which approach will work for you.

Consider your options.

Each Jewish religious movement, Reform, Reconstructionist, Conservative, and Orthodox, has its own standards for conversion. Evaluate each movement's criteria to determine its validity for you.

Understand the process.

Be certain you understand the steps of conversion at the outset of the process so that you know what will be required of you.

Consider your non-Jewish family.

Their attitude can ease—or hinder—your transition into Jewish life. Be considerate of their feelings.

When one makes the decision to convert, certain changes are bound to occur in one's life. For those who have already decided to convert, here are some suggestions from converts which may make the transition easier:

Find one rabbi to serve as your spiritual advisor.

The rabbi will guide you down the path toward conversion. You may also need a teacher. This can either be this rabbi or some other knowledgeable Jewish educator in your community. As the Talmud states, "Do not study alone. Acquire a friend." Your teacher will be a vital bridge for you to the larger Jewish community and can make the conversion process a warm, embracing experience.

Take plenty of time.

Take care to ascertain that the idea of converting is not just a passing fancy. The length of time may be different for each individual, but optimally one should have an opportunity to experience some aspects of Jewish life, and certainly *Shabbat* and some holiday celebrations. Do not try to do this under a deadline. The process should flow naturally and at a pace which is comfortable for you.

Convert for the right reasons.

As you proceed, periodically ask yourself if you are really sure about converting. Be certain that this is the right decision for *you*—a decision that will enrich your life—and that you are not converting to please (or to anger) others.

Make time for Jewish study.

Since Jewish life involves regular study, you can begin to live Jewishly by setting aside some time—even one hour—each day for Jewish study, whether it be reading a Jewish book, Jewish periodicals, or the Torah portion of the week. Begin to build a Jewish library and read as much as you can about all aspects of Judaism. Subscribe to some local and national Jewish periodicals. This will broaden your knowledge about Jewish culture, politics, religion and community. Whatever you can add to your storehouse of knowledge will help you live Jewishly. Ask to be placed on a synagogue's mailing list so you can be informed about and connected to the larger Jewish community.

Begin to "learn Judaism by doing Judaism."

You might begin by lighting *Shabbat* candles each Friday evening or by attending synagogue services every Friday evening and/or Saturday morning. Try setting aside some time on *Shabbat* for Jewish study. Start slowly, but start somewhere. Many congregations have Torah study groups, often on Saturday morning just before services.

Participate in a Jewish community.

Begin participating in the Jewish community through a synagogue, a Jewish community center, a Jewish philanthropic or social service organization (such as Hadassah, B'nai Brith, or a Jewish community federation). Share your journey with others. If you invite others who are important to you to share your new Jewish experiences, you will find that your own involvement will be more enjoyable. Your life will be enriched by these connections.

Attend synagogue on a regular basis.

The more often you attend services, the more familiar they will become. You will make new friends and will learn prayers and blessings. Their melodies will become part of your Jewish repertoire. Especially if you learn to read Hebrew, you will soon feel less and less like an "outsider."

Become acquainted with the local Jewish bookstore.

Acquire Jewish books and objects. Celebrating *Shabbat* with your own candlesticks, *kiddush* cup, and challah plate will make the experience more sweet and meaningful.

Prepare for conversion by choosing a Hebrew name.

This will be used for Jewish life-cycle and ceremonial purposes. Choosing the name is a wonderful opportunity to emulate a favorite biblical character or to honor a dear person in your family. This may be done for a non-Jewish relative by taking a Hebrew version of that name, if appropriate. Your rabbi or teacher can assist you in this decision.

Plan the actual day of conversion carefully—it will transform your life.

Take the day off from work. Surround yourself with supportive, loving family and friends. Create a spiritual environment on conversion-day. Perhaps have a celebratory meal and a reflective stroll—alone or with close friends and family. Perhaps record in a journal your thoughts about the day, the names of those on your *bet din* and those who were present for your *mikveh*.

Be patient!

Don't expect to know everything immediately or perfectly. Take things slowly, but with good feelings about the steps you take along the way. It's okay to make mistakes and to realize that you will be adding to your Jewish observance as time goes by. The most important thing is to *enjoy* the journey.

For those who have already converted, the advice offered below, which was written by Daniel, a Jew-by-Choice whose story appears in Section IV, is meant to encourage and give direction about how to proceed *after* conversion. It is hoped that his advice will help you move forward in this new phase of your lives. For those who counsel converts, perhaps Daniel's ideas will help you offer suggestions and guidance to those who have completed conversion.

Join a synagogue in which you feel at home.

I went through a little "*shul*-shopping" myself. Although I was welcomed in several, I felt at home in one. That one, and that rabbi and cantor, were instrumental in giving me the support I needed for my journey home.

Don't be dissuaded by indifference or what may appear to be antagonism.

It merely reflects a form of love that would seek to keep you from being hurt in a way that many of these people who spoke to me were hurt in their lives.

Concentrate on one aspect of Judaism.

I became intrigued with the *Midrash* and the *Pirke Avot*, the "Ethics of the Fathers." They became a source of unending joy and comfort and "welded" me to the Jewish people. From them, I was able to expand my horizons to encompass all that I needed to know to convert and eventually to celebrate a *bar mitzvah*.

Surround yourself with those who love what you love about Judaism.

With them, the path is easier.

Recognize potential family problems and face them.

I worried unnecessarily for over a year before telling my mother of my choice, for I was bound by the Torah's proscription against hurting one's parent. When I finally told her, she was completely unsurprised and scolded me a little for my hesitancy: "Don't you know me well enough to know that I believe that all roads can lead to God?"

Trust your heart.
I found that if I took the time to listen to what my heart was hearing, I was always led in the right direction.

Don't get carried away with your excitement of each new Jewish fact.
But keep that excitement alive, for you will inevitably find some way to demonstrate it to everyone. Remember that once you convert, everyone who knows of your decision will be more than a trifle curious. Even several years after my conversion, I still find that people at work express some comment or surprise about Judaism. We become representatives for Jews everywhere. This has never caused any difficulty, but it does require me to remember that I am a Jew.

To these insights, we add the following:

We hope that spouses of Jews-by-Choice will support their partners' observances of Jewish life. Attending synagogue, participating in *Shabbat*, attending lectures about current Jewish topics, celebrating the holidays in a joyful manner—all are helpful, positive ways to enrich not only your partner's Jewish life, but your religious life, as well. We have seen, time and again, that it is difficult to travel this path alone. With help from loved ones, the convert can make Judaism a reality. And your relationship can be enriched by celebrating Judaism together.

The same advice is sound for the extended families—both Jewish and non-Jewish—of those who convert to Judaism. You will find new and unexpected lines of communication and attachment as you share the experience of the convert. It does not mean that you have to embrace Judaism, but whatever you can do to learn along with the Jew-by-Choice in your family will enhance all your lives.

For the larger Jewish community, we strongly urge making Judaism *accessible* to converts and to the conversionary family. Often, this involves making extra time for them. If rabbis, whose lives are already overflowing with efforts on behalf of others, view this commitment as unfeasible, find knowledgeable lay Jews who can augment your work. They can be available for counseling, for giving follow-up workshops and classes, for offering their homes for holiday and *Shabbat* celebrations, and for being the "extended families" which many Jews-by-Choice lack.

Accessibility may also involve monetary accommodation by the Jewish establishment. Often, the newly converted do not have the means to pay a congregation's full dues. To assist them, a congregation might consider offering them a year's free membership or perhaps an initial period of reduced fees as a way to make them feel welcome. Even such little things as paying for their *mikveh,* which might cost $25, is a kindness. Some synagogues offer a year's subscription to the local Jewish newspaper. Others match new converts up for one year with others who have already converted, to help ease them through the rough spots. Some communities have committees that welcome Jews-by-Choice and their families and invite them to participate in communal activities and leadership programs. Making it financially, socially, and psychologically possible for Jews-by-Choice to "connect" following their conversion is not only good for converts. It is a "long-term investment" for the entire Jewish community and truly an expression of *tikkun olam* (repairing the world) and *chesed* (lovingkindness).

To the Jew-by-Choice, here is a final word to assist you in completing this important life-passage: Life is lived in the details. If you can continue to fill your days with the observances of Judaism, then your conversion will continue to hold its wonder for you. Even the *little* things you do on a daily basis will reinforce what you have learned. And what you have learned, you can share with the rest of the Jewish community as no one else can. Your perspective is unique and precious. Just as you need us, please know that we also need you. We are equal partners, each taking from and giving to the other. When all is said and done, remember that we stand together at Sinai, embracing the same covenant.

The following organizations can provide you with information on conversion in the form of booklets, pamphlets and guidance. Since most congregations offer an Introduction to Judaism class (as well as many other forms of adult Jewish education), as a first step in the conversion process, these organizations can refer you to those resources near you.

Another way you can make your first step toward finding out more about Judaism is to call a congregation in your area. These are usually listed in your Yellow Pages under the heading of "Synagogues."

Bear in mind that there are four main branches of Judaism in the United States: Reform, Reconstructionist, Conservative and Orthodox. Also, a few congregations call themselves "unaffiliated," "independent" or "post-denominational," or may align themselves with the Jewish Renewal movement. These invariably fall within the liberal end of Judaism's theological spectrum.

CCAR Committee on *Gerut*
Central Conference of American Rabbis (Reform Judaism)
192 Lexington Avenue
New York, NY 10016
(212) 684-4990

RRA Commission on *Gerut*
Reconstructionist Rabbinical Association
Church Road and Greenwood Avenue
Wyncote, PA 19095
(215) 576-5210

RA Committee on *Keruv*
Rabbinical Assembly of America (Conservative Judaism)
3080 Broadway
New York, NY 10027
(212) 678-8060

RCA Commission on *Gerut*
Rabbinical Council of America (Orthodox Judaism)
305 Seventh Avenue
New York, NY 10001
(212) 807-9042

OUTREACH PROGRAMS

Union of American Hebrew Congregations (Reform)
838 Fifth Avenue
New York, NY 10021
(212) 249-0100
The New York headquarters houses the National Commission of
Reform Jewish Outreach, plus the Outreach office for New York
City, Westchester and Long Island. Each of the eleven regional
offices of the UAHC also has an Outreach coordinator:

Boston: (617) 449-0404

Chicago: (312) 782-1477

Cleveland: (216) 831-6722

Dallas: (214) 960-6641

Los Angeles: (213) 653-9962

Miami: (305) 592-4792

New Jersey/Hudson Valley: (201) 599-0080

Philadelphia: (215) 563-8183

San Francisco: (415) 392-7080

Toronto: (905) 709-2275

Washington, D.C.: (202) 232-4242

United Synagogue of Conservative Judaism

155 Fifth Avenue
New York, NY 10010
(212) 533-7800
Regional offices can also provide information about appropriate
programs:

Albany, NY: (518) 438-2052

Boston: (617) 964-8210

Chicago: (312) 726-1802

Cleveland: (216) 751-0606

Connecticut: (203) 563-5531

Dallas: (214) 239-1951

Los Angeles: (310) 472-1521

Miami: (305) 474-4606

Minneapolis: (612) 920-7068

Montreal: (514) 484-4415

New Jersey: (908) 925-3114

Pacific Northwest Region: (503) 242-2328

Philadelphia: (215) 635-9701

San Francisco: (415) 377-0380

Toronto: (905) 738-1717

Washington, D.C.: (301) 230-0801

Or you can call a toll-free number for information about such
programs as Introduction to Judaism classes:
(800) ASK-N-LEARN (275-6532).

ALEPH: Alliance for Jewish Renewal

7318 Germantown Avenue
Philadelphia, PA 19119-1793
(215) 242-4074 / (215) 247-9700

Jewish Outreach Institute
333 W. 42nd St.
New York, NY 10036
(212) 642-2181
fax: (212) 642-1988
E-mail: JOI4all@aol.com
Internet: http:/wwwuser.gc.cuny.edu/cjs/joi.htm

Most congregations have support groups for interfaith couples and Jews-by-Choice. Consult a congregation in your area. On the East Coast, there is a support organization for converts:

Jewish Converts Network
1112 Hagys Ford Road
Narberth, PA 19072
(610) 664-8112
Attention: Lena Romanoff

STUDY AND LEARN: RECOMMENDED READINGS

SEARCHING FOR GOD AND SPIRITUALITY

Dresner, Samuel L. *I Asked for Wonder: A Spiritual Anthology, Abraham Joshua Heschel.* New York: The Crossroad Publishing Co. Inc., 1993. Evocative and spiritually enlightening.

Gordis, Daniel. *God Was Not in the Fire: The Search for a Spiritual Judaism.* New York: Scribner, 1995. Examines modern Jewish belief and offers ways to feel God's presence in daily life.

Heschel, Abraham Joshua. *The Sabbath: Its Meaning for Modern Man.* New York: Farrar, Straus & Giroux, 1995. A profound meditation on the nature and celebration of the Sabbath as a "cathedral in time."

Klagsbrun, Francine. *Voices of Wisdom: Jewish Ideals and Ethics for Everyday Living.* Middle Village, New York: Jonathan David Publishers Inc., 1980. An anthology of passages from Jewish sources and a guide to living in today's world.

Kushner, Harold. *Who Needs God?* New York: Summit Books, 1989. A spiritual primer. Addresses such issues as God's relevance, unlocking spirituality, the importance of religion.

Kushner, Lawrence. *God Was in This Place & I, i Did Not Know: Finding Self, Spirituality and Ultimate Meaning.* Woodstock, Vt.: Jewish Lights Publishing, 1994. Applies theological insights from Jewish mysticism to the present day.

Kushner, Lawrence. *Honey from the Rock: An Introduction to Jewish Mysticism,* Special Anniversary Edition. Woodstock, Vt.: Jewish Lights Publishing, 2000. Explains the ten gates of Jewish mysticism and how they apply to daily life.

Telushkin, Joseph. *Jewish Wisdom: Ethical, Spiritual and Historical Lessons from the Great Works and Thinkers.* New York: William Morrow & Co, Inc., 1994. Insights for living today, drawn from a comprehensive selection of passages from Jewish sources.

Waskow, Arthur. *Godwrestling—Round 2: Ancient Wisdom, Future Paths.* Woodstock, Vt.: Jewish Lights Publishing, 1998. A leader of the Jewish Renewal movement explores how Judaism relates to family, education, feminism, politics, and other aspects of our society today.

Wolpe, David. *The Healer of Shattered Hearts: A Jewish View of God.* New York: Henry Holt & Co., 1990. Invites the modern Jew to connect with the sacred by examining selections from Midrash, Bible, and Talmud.

THE APPEALS OF JUDAISM

Alpert, Rebecca T. and Jacob J. Staub. *Exploring Judaism: A Reconstructionist Approach.* Wyncote, Pa.: The Reconstructionist

Press, 1988. A clear and welcoming introduction to the beliefs and practices of Reconstructionist Judaism.

Jacobs, Louis. *The Book of Jewish Belief.* West Orange, N.J.: Behrman House, Inc., 1984. A beautifully designed introduction to basic Jewish concepts: God, Torah, *mitzvot*, Chosen People, Israel, Holocaust, Messiah and much more.

Kertzer, Morris M., rev. by Lawrence A. Hoffman. *What Is a Jew?: A Guide to the Beliefs, Traditions and Practices of Judaism That Answers Questions for Both Jew and Non-Jew.* New York: Collier Books, 1993. Revised edition of an enduring classic, which answers more than 100 commonly asked questions about Jewish life and customs.

Kling, Simcha. *Embracing Judaism.* New York: The Rabbinical Assembly, 1987. A basic introduction to Judaism, including rituals, values, history, holy days, worship and life cycle events.

Kukoff, Lydia. *Choosing Judaism.* New York: Hippocrene Books, 1981. Through the story of her own conversion journey, Kukoff conveys the joys and pitfalls experienced by converts.

Kushner, Harold. *To Life! A Celebration of Jewish Being and Thinking.* Boston: Little, Brown & Co., 1993. Jewish religious traditions, practices, and beliefs presented with humor and great spiritual insight.

Prager, Dennis and Joseph Telushkin. *The Nine Questions People Ask About Judaism.* New York: Simon & Schuster, 1986. Frank answers to major questions asked about Judaism.

Steinberg, Milton. *Basic Judaism.* New York: Harcourt Brace Jovanovich, 1965. The classic—and best—basic introduction to Jewish philosophy and theology.

JOURNEYS TO JUDAISM

Cowan, Paul. *An Orphan in History.* New York: Doubleday, 1982. One man's life-changing odyssey into his Jewish past.

Lamm, Maurice. *Becoming a Jew.* Middle Village, N.Y.: Jonathan David Publishers, Inc., 1991. Explores the traditional approach regarding converting to Judaism, and the spiritual path of the convert.

Lester, Julius. *Lovesong: Becoming a Jew.* New York: Henry Holt & Co., 1988. Traces the conversion to Judaism by an eloquent writer, the son of a Southern black Methodist minister.

Myrowitz, Catherine Hall. *Finding a Home for the Soul.* Northvale, N.J.: Jason Aronson, 1995. An in-depth sociological analysis of converts and their journeys.

Romanoff, Lena. *Your People, My People: Finding Acceptance and Fulfillment as a Jew by Choice.* Philadelphia: The Jewish Publication Society of America, 1990. A convert to Judaism and the director of the Jewish Converts Network offers insights into the choices and challenges confronting those who convert.

Scalamonti, John David. *Ordained To Be a Jew.* Hoboken, N.J.: Ktav Publishing House, Inc., 1992. The fascinating story of an ordained Catholic priest's search for spirituality and how he found it in Judaism.

TURNING FAITH INTO ACTION

Artson, Bradley Shavit. *It's a Mitzvah: Step-by-Step to Jewish Living.* West Orange, N.J.: Behrman House, Inc./The Rabbinic Assembly, 1995. A beautifully designed presentation of the essentials of Jewish observance.

Donin, Hayim Halevy. *To Be a Jew: A Guide to Jewish Observance in Contemporary Life*. New York: Basic Books, 1972. A solid review of Jewish life cycle events, holidays, and observances the year round.

Greenberg, Blu. *How to Run a Traditional Jewish Household*. New York: Simon & Schuster, 1983. A fine exploration of the whys and hows of running a Jewish home.

Greenberg, Irving. *The Jewish Way: Living the Holidays*. New York: Summit Books, 1988. A comprehensive and compelling presentation of Jewish life, explored through the holidays.

Knobel, Peter S., ed. *Gates of the Seasons: A Guide to the Jewish Year*. New York: Central Conference of American Rabbis, 1983. An outline of the *mitzvot* of the Jewish holiday cycle, written from a Reform perspective.

Siegel, Richard, Michael Strassfeld and Sharon Strassfeld, eds. *The Jewish Catalog: A Do-It-Yourself Kit*. Philadelphia: The Jewish Publication Society of America, 1973.

Strassfeld, Sharon and Michael Strassfeld, eds. *The Second Jewish Catalog: Sources & Resources*. Philadelphia: The Jewish Publication Society of America, 1976.

Strassfeld, Sharon and Michael Strassfeld, eds. *The Third Jewish Catalog: Creating Community*. Philadelphia: The Jewish Publication Society of America, 1980.
The best primers on how to/why to/when to engage in Jewish life.

Syme, Daniel B. *The Jewish Home: A Guide for Jewish Living*. New York: UAHC Press, 1988. Written in a conversational question-and-answer format, contains many valuable details and information about the meaning of customs and rituals in today's Jewish home.

Telushkin, Joseph. *Jewish Literacy: The Most Important Things to Know About the Jewish Religion, Its People, and Its History*. New York: William Morrow & Co. Inc., 1991. This book's title says it all—and its contents delivers it all. A classic in its own time.

Waskow, Arthur. *Seasons of Our Joy: A Modern Guide to the Jewish Holidays*. Boston: Beacon Press, 1982. The meaning of each Jewish holiday with particular attention to individual spirituality.

GLOSSARY

(Unless otherwise noted, all words being defined are Hebrew.)

Adonai: A primary Hebrew name of God.

Aleinu: The closing prayer of each daily service which proclaims the ultimate reign of God and the unique destiny of the Jewish people.

Aliyah: "Going up." Refers to "going up" to the Torah during services or to immigrating to Israel.

Am Yisrael: Refers to the entire entity of the Jewish People.

Barkhu: The call to worship which begins each morning and evening service. A prayer which informs the congregation to focus its attention.

Baruch atta Adonai eloheinu melekh haolam: "Blessed are You, Lord our God, King of the universe." The Hebrew phrase which begins every Jewish blessing.

Bar mitzvah (pl. b'nai mitzvah): "Son of the commandment." The age at which a Jewish boy becomes responsible for his actions. By extension, also the ceremony celebrating his achieving that status. This is generally held around his thirteenth birthday.

Bat mitzvah (*pl. *b'not mitzvah): "Daughter of the commandment." The age at which a Jewish girl becomes religiously responsible for her actions. By extension, also the ceremony celebrating her achieving that status. This is generally held around her twelfth or thirteenth birthday.

Berachah (*pl. *berachot): A blessing or benediction.

Bet din: A rabbinic court. May be convened for the purpose of overseeing a conversion ceremony, to prepare a Jewish writ of divorce or to serve as a mediating body in a dispute between two Jews.

Bimah: The dais in the sanctuary from which the Torah is read and where the leader of the service stands when leading services.

Brit: "Covenant." Often refers to the covenant between God and the Jewish people.

Brit milah: Ritual circumcision.

Chai: Life.

Daven: (Yiddish) "To pray."

Gemilut hasadim: Deeds of lovingkindness.

Ger tzedek: "Righteous convert." The traditional term for one who converts to Judaism.

Gilgul: Jewish mystics' traditional term to refer to a reincarnated soul.

Haggadah: The book of prayers, songs and stories used during the Passover *seder.*

Halakhah: Jewish law.

Hanukhat habayit: The act of dedicating a Jewish home by placing a *mezuzah* on the door.

Hanukkah: The eight-day Festival of Lights which recalls the

Maccabean victory over Greco-Syrian religious oppression. Usually falls in December.

Hatafat dam brit: Symbolic ritual circumcision. A drop of blood is drawn from the penis at the conversion ceremony of a male convert to Judaism.

Hava Nagila: A Jewish song sung at joyous celebrations.

Havurah: A "fellowship" oriented around study, celebration of Jewish holidays, spiritual development and/or social purposes.

Kabbalat Shabbat: The ritual of welcoming the Sabbath.

Kaddish: A prayer of praise to God recited for almost a year after the death of a close relative and on the anniversary of that person's death.

Kashrut: Jewish dietary laws.

Kavannah: Heartfelt concentration and devotion which accompanies the recitation of prayers.

Kippah: The ritual headcovering. Also called by its Yiddish name, *yarmulke.*

Ki vanu vacharta: "For You have chosen us." An expression from the prayer which sanctifies the Sabbath.

Klal Yisrael: Refers to the collective entity of the Jewish People.

Kosher: Food which conforms to the Jewish dietary laws.

Kotel: The Western Wall in Jerusalem, the last remaining section of the Second Temple.

L'chaim: "To life." Used as a celebratory toast and to bestow good wishes on another person.

Mashgiach: One who supervises the preparation of kosher food.

Menorah: A seven- or eight-branched candelabrum. If the latter, it is used expressly to hold Hanukkah candles.

Mezuzah: Literally, "doorpost." First two paragraphs of the *Sh'ma*, a Jewish prayer, written on a parchment scroll and encased in a small container, affixed to the doorposts of a Jewish home.

Midrash: Rabbinic commentaries on the Bible.

Mikveh: A ritual bath used (among other things) in the conversion ceremony.

Minyan: A minimum of 10 individuals required to recite certain communal prayers.

Mitzvah (pl. **mitzvot):** Behavior commanded by God or mandated by Jewish tradition.

Nefesh: Soul.

Oneg Shabbat: Literally, "Sabbath joy." Usually refers to a fellowship hour which follows Friday evening services.

Oseh Shalom: "Creator of Peace."

Pesach: Passover, the holiday celebrating the Exodus of the Israelites from Egypt.

Pirke Avot: Literally "Chapters of the Fathers," but often referred to as "Ethics of the Fathers." A collection of pithy sayings from the Talmudic era, about 200 B.C.E.-500 C.E.

Rosh Chodesh: The celebration of the new month.

Rosh Hashanah: The Jewish New Year. Usually falls in September or October.

Ruach: Spirit. Usually refers to a mystical sense of one's "spirit."

Seder: The home-based ceremony held on the first two nights of Passover.

Shabbat: The Sabbath.

Shalom: "Hello." "Goodbye." "Peace."

Shehecheyanu: The blessing recited for the observance of a joyous happening.

Sh'ma: The central statement of belief in One God. The full statement is *"Sh'ma Yisrael Adonai Eloheinu Adonai Echad"*—"Hear, O Israel, the Lord Our God, the Lord is One."

Shofar: A ram's horn. Usually sounded on Rosh Hashanah.

Shomer kashrut: One who observes the laws of *kashrut*.

Shul: (Yiddish) Synagogue.

Siddur: Prayerbook.

Simcha: A joyful celebration.

Tanakh: The Hebrew Bible, comprised of three sections: *Torah* (the Five Books of Moses), *Nevi'im* (The Prophets), and *Ketuvim* (The Writings, such as Psalms, Proverbs and Job).

Tefillah: Prayer.

Tekiah: One of the notes sounded on the *shofar*.

Tikkun olam: "Repairing the world" to make it a better place.

Tisha B'Av: Commemorates the destruction of the First and Second Temples, a major fast day during the Jewish year. Usually falls in July or August.

Torah: The Five Books of Moses.

Tu B'shvat: The Jewish arbor day. Usually falls in January or February.

Tzedakah: Acts of righteousness performed through monetary donations.

Tzedek: Righteousness.

V'ahavta: Deuteronomy 6:4-9, which affirms that God alone is to be our God and instructs the Jew how to make this teaching the guidepost of our daily life. Recited in conjunction with the *Sh'ma*.

Yom Hashoah: Holocaust Memorial Day. Usually falls in April or May.

Yom Kippur: Day of Atonement. Usually falls in September or October.

MAJOR CONTRIBUTORS

AHARON

Aharon is a 43-year-old poet who sat alone in an airport control tower and contemplated the Divine. Raised as a Roman Catholic, his spiritual search led him to Judaism. He describes himself as a "writer and communicator dedicated to helping people develop and enrich their spiritual relationship with Judaism." He has just been accepted to Conservative rabbinical school.

DANIEL

Raised as a Roman Catholic, Daniel converted to Judaism two years ago at the age of 48. A retired U.S. Navy Commander, with a graduate degree from M.I.T. in analytical engineering, his approach to Judaism was primarily intellectual. He is regional vice president of a major audio-visual systems integrating company. His current Jewish activities involve participating in a Torah study group and belonging to a large Reform synagogue.

ELISHEVA

Elisheva converted almost seven years ago at the age of 22. She has a Jewish father and a Catholic mother. She considers Jewish peoplehood to be the foundation of cultural, religious and ethical Jewish living.

ELISHEVA TZIPORA

Elisheva Tzipora's background is Swedish-Polish-Israeli as well as Jewish/non-Jewish. Her father's side of the family included such Jewish luminaries as Rabbi Levi Yitzhak of Berditchev. She was 30 years old when she converted. Married to an Israeli whose father is from South Africa and whose mother is a sixth-generation Jerusalemite, she is the mother of a young son and is working toward a Ph.D. in social and communal systems.

MICHAEL

Michael, who is 50 years old, felt the first "stirrings" of wanting to be Jewish when he was in high school. He survived combat in Vietnam. Through "chance" acquaintances, he eventually found himself in an environment that supported his pursuit of Jewish knowledge. His conversion took place a year and a half later. He is now an active member of a Conservative synagogue, where he engages in Torah study. He is looking forward to his second trip to Israel.

MIRIAM

Miriam was born in Germany during World War II. Her father was Jewish; her mother was a non-Jew. Raised as a Protestant, her conversion to Judaism took place when she was 44 years old. Miriam grapples with "what my people, the Germans, did to my people, the Jews."

MIRIAM HANNAH

All her life, Miriam Hannah considered herself to be a Jew. She was raised with Jewish holidays and customs, attended synagogue and lived a Jewish life, never questioning her identity. Just before her marriage, she discovered that, according to Jewish religious law, she was not Jewish because, even though her father was a Jew, her mother was not. After marrying a non-Jew and having two daughters in her late twenties, she formalized a religious status which had been in her heart for many years. She is now active in Jewish causes and belongs to her childhood synagogue.

NAFSHIYA

Although Nafshiya grew up in a home where no religion was strictly observed, she was drawn to Judaism from a very early age: "I felt envy toward those who were Jews—the strong sense of family, direction, and discipline were all attractive elements to me. They still are." She formally converted to Judaism when she was 36 years old. Now married to a Jew, she is the mother of a baby boy.

NAOMI DEVORAH

Naomi Devorah was 27 years old when she converted to Judaism. She is an attorney and teaches law at a community college. She and her husband belong to a large Reform synagogue and have two young children.

OMRI

Omri was 32 when he converted. He was raised as a Catholic, but felt spiritually constricted by his church. First as a Coast Guard medic, and now as a charge nurse in the emergency room of a large county hospital, he has repeatedly faced danger and death. His search for religious meaning and spiritual freedom led him to Judaism.

RENATYA

Renatya completed her conversion to Judaism at the age of 27. Born in communist Czechoslovakia, where she had no religious upbringing, she discovered Judaism when she came to America. Now a physician, she and her husband were recently married by his childhood rabbi in a Washington, D.C. suburb.

RINA

Rina, who was raised an Episcopalian, converted to Judaism when she was 33. An actress, she is married and has two children. She is helping to establish a new synagogue.

SARAH

At the age of 40, Sarah decided to convert to Judaism. A scholar with advanced degrees in Asian religions and in non-profit management, she had sought her spiritual home as far away as Japan before returning to the United States and finding her "home" in Judaism. Now married, she is working on a Ph.D. in higher education.

SHOSHANA

Shoshana was 27 years old when she completed her conversion. She came from Taiwan to the West Coast of the United States, where she earned a degree in engineering. Her husband, who is Jewish, escaped with his family from Iran in the 1970s. They have two daughters and belong to a large Reform congregation in northern California.

SIMCHA

Simcha was 28 years old when she converted. She discovered Judaism while growing up in Australia. Her mother was a Roman Catholic and her father a profound atheist. Her spiritual search led her from New York to California to Jerusalem—and back again. Now a psychiatrist at a large hospital on the East Coast, she is exploring Judaism from Orthodox to Reform. Her goal is to integrate Jewish spiritual insights with the discipline of modern psychology.

YAAKOVA

Yaakova, an African-American raised as a Unitarian, was 36 years old when she converted to Judaism. A physician, she is dedicated to spiritual and physical healing.

YONATON

Born in Canada and raised in the eastern part of the United States, Yonaton grew up in a home with no formal religion. He fell in love with a young woman who introduced him to Jewish life. This inspired him to pursue a course of study toward conversion. At the age of 25, he became a Jew. He is pursuing a Ph.D. in Slavic languages and literature at a large California university. He also sings in the choir of the synagogue to which he and his wife belong.

YOSEF

Yosef survived a tough Brooklyn childhood, enlisted in the Navy and ended up on the West Coast where he fell in love with a Jewish girl. This relationship brought him a bride, a new family and a new outlook on life. At the age of 28, he "came home" to Judaism, which he says was like coming "at long last, into a safe harbor." He is currently earning his degree in occupational therapy. He greatly enjoys attending services at both a Reform synagogue and at the Conservative synagogue where his wife grew up.

ZAKIYA

Zakiya was 38 years old when she converted. She is divorced and the single mother of three children. Since her conversion, she has been trying to find ways to integrate Judaism into the life of her family. In connection with her profession as a radiology nurse, she is exploring the healing aspects of Judaism, serves on the board of a Jewish hospice and has prepared bodies for burial as part of her local "*Hevra Kadisha*," the Jewish burial society.

ACKNOWLEDGMENTS

WE WISH TO THANK THE MANY PEOPLE WHO HELPED TO make this book a reality.

First and foremost, our thanks go to Stuart Matlins, our dedicated publisher, who perceived the vision of this project and had faith in its ultimate realization. Without his patient support, our efforts could not have come to fruition. To Sandra Korinchak, Antoinette Matlins and the entire staff of Jewish Lights Publishing, we are most grateful for their expertise in reading the many drafts of the manuscript and for providing insight and valuable suggestions. To our gifted and meticulous editor, Arthur Magida, we extend our heartfelt gratitude. No one could have been blessed with a finer craftsman. He cleared his way through the thicket of our words and brought them to flower.

To our students, whose words illuminate these pages, we owe a great debt. Without their willingness to share their lives with us and with you, the reader, this book would have remained a vague dream. They are the true "authors," and we thank them for sharing their stories so that we all might learn from them. (As

Maimonides once said, "From all my teachers I have gotten understanding, but from my students most of all.")

To our families: Larry Moskovitz, Jeff and Sarah Moskovitz, Dan and Kim Moskovitz, Debbi and Ron Seligman, and Rebecca Mia Seligman; Mindy Berkowitz, Elisha and Eitan Berkowitz, Rebecca and Abigail Goodman—we thank you for your unending patience over months of long hours and for your helpful suggestions during the many phases and drafts of this book. We owe a special thanks to Jeff and Sarah, the "computer-geniuses" par excellence, who were always there to help us when we most needed it. Without their diligence and knowledge, this manuscript would never have reached the publisher.

To Rabbi Marv Goodman, we thank you for bringing the two of us together to work on this project. It was a wonderful *"shidduch"* ("match")!

We thank God for granting us the opportunity to write this book, and we ask that God bless the work of our hands and the fruit of our labors.

—Rabbi Allan L. Berkowitz
—Patti Moskovitz
14 Iyar 5756
Parashat Emor

Notes

Notes

Notes

Notes

Notes

Notes

Notes

Notes

Notes

Notes

Bar/Bat Mitzvah

The Bar/Bat Mitzvah Memory Book
An Album for Treasuring the Spiritual Celebration
By Rabbi Jeffrey K. Salkin and Nina Salkin
A unique album for preserving the spiritual memories of the day, and for recording plans for the Jewish future ahead. Contents include space for creating or recording family history; teachings received from rabbi, cantor, and others; mitzvot and *tzedakot* chosen and carried out, etc.
8 x 10, 48 pp, Deluxe Hardcover, 2-color text, ribbon marker, ISBN 1-58023-111-X **$19.95**

Bar/Bat Mitzvah Basics: A Practical Family Guide to Coming of Age Together
Edited by Helen Leneman. Foreword by Rabbi Jeffrey K. Salkin.
6 x 9, 240 pp, Quality PB, ISBN 1-58023-151-9 **$18.95**

For Kids—Putting God on Your Guest List: How to Claim the Spiritual Meaning of Your Bar or Bat Mitzvah *By Rabbi Jeffrey K. Salkin*
6 x 9, 144 pp, Quality PB, ISBN 1-58023-015-6 **$14.95** *For ages 11–12*

Putting God on the Guest List: How to Reclaim the Spiritual Meaning of Your Child's Bar or Bat Mitzvah *By Rabbi Jeffrey K. Salkin*
6 x 9, 224 pp, Quality PB, ISBN 1-879045-59-1 **$16.95**

Tough Questions Jews Ask: A Young Adult's Guide to Building a Jewish Life
By Rabbi Edward Feinstein 6 x 9, 160 pp, Quality PB, ISBN 1-58023-139-X **$14.95** *For ages 13 & up*
Also Available: **Tough Questions Jews Ask Teacher's Guide**
8½ x 11, 72 pp, PB, ISBN 1-58023-187-X **$8.95**

Bible Study/Midrash

Hineini in Our Lives: Learning How to Respond to Others through 14 Biblical Texts, and Personal Stories *By Norman J. Cohen*
6 x 9, 240 pp, Hardcover, ISBN 1-58023-131-4 **$23.95**

Ancient Secrets: Using the Stories of the Bible to Improve Our Everyday Lives
By Rabbi Levi Meier, Ph.D. 5½ x 8½, 288 pp, Quality PB, ISBN 1-58023-064-4 **$16.95**

Moses—The Prince, the Prophet: His Life, Legend & Message for Our Lives
By Rabbi Levi Meier, Ph.D.
6 x 9, 224 pp, Quality PB, ISBN 1-58023-069-5 **$16.95**

Self, Struggle & Change: Family Conflict Stories in Genesis and Their Healing Insights for Our Lives *By Norman J. Cohen* 6 x 9, 224 pp, Quality PB, ISBN 1-879045-66-4 **$18.99**

Voices from Genesis: Guiding Us through the Stages of Life *By Norman J. Cohen*
6 x 9, 192 pp, Quality PB, ISBN 1-58023-118-7 **$16.95**

Congregation Resources

Becoming a Congregation of Learners: Learning as a Key to Revitalizing Congregational Life *By Isa Aron, Ph.D. Foreword by Rabbi Lawrence A. Hoffman.*
6 x 9, 304 pp, Quality PB, ISBN 1-58023-089-X **$19.95**

Finding a Spiritual Home: How a New Generation of Jews Can Transform the American Synagogue *By Rabbi Sidney Schwarz*
6 x 9, 352 pp, Quality PB, ISBN 1-58023-185-3 **$19.95**

Jewish Pastoral Care: A Practical Handbook from Traditional & Contemporary Sources
Edited by Rabbi Dayle A. Friedman 6 x 9, 464 pp, Hardcover, ISBN 1-58023-078-4 **$35.00**

The Self-Renewing Congregation: Organizational Strategies for Revitalizing Congregational Life *By Isa Aron, Ph.D. Foreword by Dr. Ron Wolfson.*
6 x 9, 304 pp, Quality PB, ISBN 1-58023-166-7 **$19.95**

Or phone, fax, mail or e-mail to: **JEWISH LIGHTS Publishing**
Sunset Farm Offices, Route 4 • P.O. Box 237 • Woodstock, Vermont 05091
Tel: (802) 457-4000 • Fax: (802) 457-4004 • www.jewishlights.com
Credit card orders: **(800) 962-4544** (8:30AM–5:30PM ET Monday–Friday)
Generous discounts on quantity orders. SATISFACTION GUARANTEED. Prices subject to change.

Children's Books

What You Will See Inside a Synagogue
By Rabbi Lawrence A. Hoffman and Dr. Ron Wolfson; Full-color photos by Bill Aron

A colorful, fun-to-read introduction that explains the ways and whys of Jewish worship and religious life. Full-page photos; concise but informative descriptions of the objects used, the clergy and laypeople who have specific roles, and much more.

8½ x 10½, 32 pp, Full-color photos, Hardcover, ISBN 1-59473-012-1 **$17.99** *(A SkyLight Paths book)*

Because Nothing Looks Like God
By Lawrence and Karen Kushner

What is God like? Introduces children to the possibilities of spiritual life. Real-life examples of happiness and sadness invite us to explore, together with our children, the questions we all have about God.

11 x 8½, 32 pp, Full-color illus., Hardcover, ISBN 1-58023-092-X **$16.95** *For ages 4 & up*

Also Available: **Because Nothing Looks Like God Teacher's Guide**
8½ x 11, 22 pp, PB, ISBN 1-58023-140-3 **$6.95** *For ages 5–8*

Board Book Companions to *Because Nothing Looks Like God*
5 x 5, 24 pp, Full-color illus., SkyLight Paths Board Books, **$7.95** each *For ages 0–4*

What Does God Look Like? ISBN 1-893361-23-3

How Does God Make Things Happen? ISBN 1-893361-24-1

Where Is God? ISBN 1-893361-17-9

The 11th Commandment: Wisdom from Our Children
by The Children of America

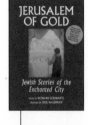

"If there were an Eleventh Commandment, what would it be?" Children of many religious denominations across America answer in their own drawings and words.

8 x 10, 48 pp, Full-color illus., Hardcover, ISBN 1-879045-46-X **$16.95** *For all ages*

Jerusalem of Gold: Jewish Stories of the Enchanted City
Retold by Howard Schwartz. Full-color illus. by Neil Waldman.

A beautiful and engaging collection of historical and legendary stories for children. Based on Talmud, midrash, Jewish folklore, and mystical and Hasidic sources.

8 x 10, 64 pp, Full-color illus., Hardcover, ISBN 1-58023-149-7 **$18.95** *For ages 7 & up*

The Book of Miracles: A Young Person's Guide to Jewish Spiritual Awareness
By Lawrence Kushner. All-new illustrations by the author.

6 x 9, 96 pp, 2-color illus., Hardcover, ISBN 1-879045-78-8 **$16.95** *For ages 9–13*

In Our Image: God's First Creatures
By Nancy Sohn Swartz

9 x 12, 32 pp, Full-color illus., Hardcover, ISBN 1-879045-99-0 **$16.95** *For ages 4 & up*

Also Available as a Board Book: **How Did the Animals Help God?**
5 x 5, 24 pp, Board, Full-color illus., ISBN 1-59473-044-X **$7.99** *For ages 0–4 (A SkyLight Paths book)*

From SKYLIGHT PATHS PUBLISHING

Becoming Me: A Story of Creation
By Martin Boroson. Full-color illus. by Christopher Gilvan-Cartwright.

Told in the personal "voice" of the Creator, a story about creation and relationship that is about each one of us.

8 x 10, 32 pp, Full-color illus., Hardcover, ISBN 1-893361-11-X **$16.95** *For ages 4 & up*

Ten Amazing People: And How They Changed the World
By Maura D. Shaw. Foreword by Dr. Robert Coles. Full-color illus. by Stephen Marchesi.

Black Elk • Dorothy Day • Malcolm X • Mahatma Gandhi • Martin Luther King, Jr. • Mother Teresa • Janusz Korczak • Desmond Tutu • Thich Nhat Hanh • Albert Schweitzer.

8½ x 11, 48 pp, Full-color illus., Hardcover, ISBN 1-893361-47-0 **$17.95** *For ages 7 & up*

Where Does God Live? *By August Gold and Matthew J. Perlman*

Helps young readers develop a personal understanding of God.

10 x 8½ , 32 pp, Full-color photo illus., Quality PB, ISBN 1-893361-39-X **$8.99** *For ages 3–6*

Children's Books
by Sandy Eisenberg Sasso

Adam & Eve's First Sunset: God's New Day
Engaging new story explores fear and hope, faith and gratitude in ways that will delight kids and adults—inspiring us to bless each of God's days and nights.
9 x 12, 32 pp, Full-color illus., Hardcover, ISBN 1-58023-177-2 **$17.95** *For ages 4 & up*

But God Remembered
Stories of Women from Creation to the Promised Land
Four different stories of women—Lillith, Serach, Bityah, and the Daughters of Z—teach us important values through their faith and actions.
9 x 12, 32 pp, Full-color illus., Hardcover, ISBN 1-879045-43-5 **$16.95** *For ages 8 & up*

Cain & Abel: Finding the Fruits of Peace
Shows children that we have the power to deal with anger in positive ways. Provides questions for kids and adults to explore together.
9 x 12, 32 pp, Full-color illus., Hardcover, ISBN 1-58023-123-3 **$16.95** *For ages 5 & up*

God in Between
If you wanted to find God, where would you look? This magical, mythical tale teaches that God can be found where we are: within all of us and the relationships between us.
9 x 12, 32 pp, Full-color illus., Hardcover, ISBN 1-879045-86-9 **$16.95** *For ages 4 & up*

God's Paintbrush: Special 10th Anniversary Edition
Wonderfully interactive, invites children of all faiths and backgrounds to encounter God through moments in their own lives. Provides questions adult and child can explore together.
11 x 8½, 32 pp, Full-color illus., Hardcover, ISBN 1-58023-195-0 **$17.95** *For ages 4 & up*

Also Available: God's Paintbrush Teacher's Guide
8½ x 11, 32 pp, PB, ISBN 1-879045-57-5 **$8.95**

God's Paintbrush Celebration Kit
A Spiritual Activity Kit for Teachers and Students of All Faiths, All Backgrounds
Additional activity sheets available:
8-Student Activity Sheet Pack (40 sheets/5 sessions), ISBN 1-58023-058-X **$19.95**
Single-Student Activity Sheet Pack (5 sessions), ISBN 1-58023-059-8 **$3.95**

In God's Name
Like an ancient myth in its poetic text and vibrant illustrations, this award-winning modern fable about the search for God's name celebrates the diversity and, at the same time, the unity of all people.
9 x 12, 32 pp, Full-color illus., Hardcover, ISBN 1-879045-26-5 **$16.99** *For ages 4 & up*

Also Available as a Board Book: What Is God's Name?
5 x 5, 24 pp, Board, Full-color illus., ISBN 1-893361-10-1 **$7.99** *For ages 0–4 (A SkyLight Paths book)*

Also Available: In God's Name video and study guide
Computer animation, original music, and children's voices. 18 min. **$29.99**

Also Available in Spanish: El nombre de Dios
9 x 12, 32 pp, Full-color illus., Hardcover, ISBN 1-893361-63-2 **$16.95** *(A SkyLight Paths book)*

Noah's Wife: The Story of Naamah
When God tells Noah to bring the animals of the world onto the ark, God also calls on Naamah, Noah's wife, to save each plant on Earth. Based on an ancient text.
9 x 12, 32 pp, Full-color illus., Hardcover, ISBN 1-58023-134-9 **$16.95** *For ages 4 & up*

Also Available as a Board Book: Naamah, Noah's Wife
5 x 5, 24 pp, Full-color illus., Board, ISBN 1-893361-56-X **$7.95** *For ages 0–4 (A SkyLight Paths book)*

For Heaven's Sake: Finding God in Unexpected Places
9 x 12, 32 pp, Full-color illus., Hardcover, ISBN 1-58023-054-7 **$16.95** *For ages 4 & up*

God Said Amen: Finding the Answers to Our Prayers
9 x 12, 32 pp, Full-color illus., Hardcover, ISBN 1-58023-080-6 **$16.95** *For ages 4 & up*

Current Events/History

The Story of the Jews: A 4,000-Year Adventure—A Graphic History Book
Written & illustrated by Stan Mack
Through witty, illustrated narrative, we visit all the major happenings from biblical times to the twenty-first century. Celebrates the major characters and events that have shaped the Jewish people and culture.
6 x 9, 288 pp, illus., Quality PB, ISBN 1-58023-155-1 **$16.95**

The Jewish Prophet: Visionary Words from Moses and Miriam to Henrietta Szold and A. J. Heschel *By Rabbi Michael J. Shire*
6½ x 8½, 128 pp, 123 full-color illus., Hardcover, ISBN 1-58023-168-3 **$25.00**

Shared Dreams: Martin Luther King, Jr. & the Jewish Community
By Rabbi Marc Schneier. Preface by Martin Luther King III.
6 x 9, 240 pp, Hardcover, ISBN 1-58023-062-8 **$24.95**

"Who Is a Jew?": Conversations, Not Conclusions *By Meryl Hyman*
6 x 9, 272 pp, Quality PB, ISBN 1-58023-052-0 **$16.95**

Ecology

Ecology & the Jewish Spirit: Where Nature & the Sacred Meet
Edited by Ellen Bernstein 6 x 9, 288 pp, Quality PB, ISBN 1-58023-082-2 **$16.95**

Torah of the Earth: Exploring 4,000 Years of Ecology in Jewish Thought
Vol. 1: Biblical Israel: One Land, One People; Rabbinic Judaism: One People, Many Lands
Vol. 2: Zionism: One Land, Two Peoples; Eco-Judaism: One Earth, Many Peoples
Edited by Rabbi Arthur Waskow
Vol. 1: 6 x 9, 272 pp, Quality PB, ISBN 1-58023-086-5 **$19.95**
Vol. 2: 6 x 9, 336 pp, Quality PB, ISBN 1-58023-087-3 **$19.95**

Grief/Healing

Against the Dying of the Light: A Parent's Story of Love, Loss and Hope
By Leonard Fein
In this unusual exploration of heartbreak and healing, Leonard Fein chronicles the sudden death of his 30-year-old daughter and shares the hard-earned wisdom that emerges in the face of loss and grief.
5½ x 8½, 176 pp, Quality PB, ISBN 1-58023-197-7 **$15.99**

Grief in Our Seasons: A Mourner's Kaddish Companion *By Rabbi Kerry M. Olitzky*
4½ x 6½, 448 pp, Quality PB, ISBN 1-879045-55-9 **$15.95**

Healing of Soul, Healing of Body: Spiritual Leaders Unfold the Strength & Solace in Psalms *Edited by Rabbi Simkha Y. Weintraub, C.S.W.*
6 x 9, 128 pp, 2-color illus. text, Quality PB, ISBN 1-879045-31-1 **$14.95**

Jewish Paths toward Healing and Wholeness: A Personal Guide to Dealing with Suffering *By Rabbi Kerry M. Olitzky. Foreword by Debbie Friedman.*
6 x 9, 192 pp, Quality PB, ISBN 1-58023-068-7 **$15.95**

Mourning & Mitzvah, 2nd Edition: A Guided Journal for Walking the Mourner's Path through Grief to Healing *By Anne Brener, L.C.S.W.*
7½ x 9, 304 pp, Quality PB, ISBN 1-58023-113-6 **$19.95**

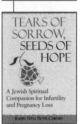

The Perfect Stranger's Guide to Funerals and Grieving Practices
A Guide to Etiquette in Other People's Religious Ceremonies *Edited by Stuart M. Matlins*
6 x 9, 240 pp, Quality PB, ISBN 1-893361-20-9 **$16.95** *(A SkyLight Paths book)*

Tears of Sorrow, Seeds of Hope: A Jewish Spiritual Companion for Infertility and Pregnancy Loss *By Rabbi Nina Beth Cardin*
6 x 9, 192 pp, Hardcover, ISBN 1-58023-017-2 **$19.95**

A Time to Mourn, A Time to Comfort: A Guide to Jewish Bereavement and Comfort *By Dr. Ron Wolfson* 7 x 9, 336 pp, Quality PB, ISBN 1-879045-96-6 **$18.95**

When a Grandparent Dies: A Kid's Own Remembering Workbook for Dealing with Shiva and the Year Beyond *By Nechama Liss-Levinson, Ph.D.*
8 x 10, 48 pp, 2-color text, Hardcover, ISBN 1-879045-44-3 **$15.95** *For ages 7–13*

Abraham Joshua Heschel

The Earth Is the Lord's: The Inner World of the Jew in Eastern Europe
5½ x 8, 128 pp, Quality PB, ISBN 1-879045-42-7 **$14.95**

Israel: An Echo of Eternity *New Introduction by Susannah Heschel*
5½ x 8, 272 pp, Quality PB, ISBN 1-879045-70-2 **$19.95**

A Passion for Truth: Despair and Hope in Hasidism
5½ x 8, 352 pp, Quality PB, ISBN 1-879045-41-9 **$18.99**

Holidays/Holy Days

Reclaiming Judaism as a Spiritual Practice: Holy Days and Shabbat
By Rabbi Goldie Milgram
Provides a framework for understanding the powerful and often unexplained intellectual, emotional, and spiritual tools that are essential for a lively, relevant, and fulfilling Jewish spiritual practice. 7 x 9, 272 pp, Quality PB, ISBN 1-58023-205-1 **$19.99**

7th Heaven: Celebrating Shabbat with Rebbe Nachman of Breslov
By Moshe Mykoff with the Breslov Research Institute
Based on the teachings of Rebbe Nachman of Breslov. Explores the art of consciously observing Shabbat and understanding in-depth many of the day's traditional spiritual practices. 5⅛ x 8¼, 224 pp, Deluxe PB w/flaps, ISBN 1-58023-175-6 **$18.95**

The Women's Passover Companion
Women's Reflections on the Festival of Freedom
Edited by Rabbi Sharon Cohen Anisfeld, Tara Mohr, and Catherine Spector
Groundbreaking. A provocative conversation about women's relationships to Passover as well as the roots and meanings of women's seders.
6 x 9, 352 pp, Hardcover, ISBN 1-58023-128-4 **$24.95**

The Women's Seder Sourcebook
Rituals & Readings for Use at the Passover Seder
Edited by Rabbi Sharon Cohen Anisfeld, Tara Mohr, and Catherine Spector
Gathers the voices of more than one hundred women in readings, personal and creative reflections, commentaries, blessings, and ritual suggestions that can be incorporated into your Passover celebration as supplements to or substitutes for traditional passages of the haggadah.
6 x 9, 384 pp, Hardcover, ISBN 1-58023-136-5 **$24.95**

Creating Lively Passover Seders: A Sourcebook of Engaging Tales, Texts & Activities
By David Arnow, Ph.D. 7 x 9, 416 pp, Quality PB, ISBN 1-58023-184-5 **$24.99**

Hanukkah, 2nd Edition: The Family Guide to Spiritual Celebration
By Dr. Ron Wolfson. Edited by Joel Lurie Grishaver.
7 x 9, 240 pp, illus., Quality PB, ISBN 1-58023-122-5 **$18.95**

The Jewish Family Fun Book: Holiday Projects, Everyday Activities, and Travel Ideas with Jewish Themes *By Danielle Dardashti and Roni Sarig. Illus. by Avi Katz.*
6 x 9, 288 pp, 70+ b/w illus. & diagrams, Quality PB, ISBN 1-58023-171-3 **$18.95**

The Jewish Gardening Cookbook: Growing Plants & Cooking for
Holidays & Festivals *By Michael Brown* 6 x 9, 224 pp, 30+ illus., Quality PB, ISBN 1-58023-116-0 **$16.95**

The Jewish Lights Book of Fun Classroom Activities: Simple and Seasonal
Projects for Teachers and Students *By Danielle Dardashti and Roni Sarig*
6 x 9, 240 pp, Quality PB, ISBN 1-58023-206-X **$19.99**

Passover, 2nd Edition: The Family Guide to Spiritual Celebration
By Dr. Ron Wolfson with Joel Lurie Grishaver 7 x 9, 352 pp, Quality PB, ISBN 1-58023-174-8 **$19.95**

Shabbat, 2nd Edition: The Family Guide to Preparing for and Celebrating the Sabbath
By Dr. Ron Wolfson 7 x 9, 320 pp, illus., Quality PB, ISBN 1-58023-164-0 **$19.95**

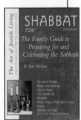

Sharing Blessings: Children's Stories for Exploring the Spirit of the Jewish Holidays
By Rahel Musleah and Michael Klayman
8½ x 11, 64 pp, Full-color illus., Hardcover, ISBN 1-879045-71-0 **$18.95** *For ages 6 & up*

Inspiration

God in All Moments
Mystical & Practical Spiritual Wisdom from Hasidic Masters
Edited and translated by Or N. Rose with Ebn D. Leader
Hasidic teachings on how to be mindful in religious practice and cultivating everyday ethical behavior—*hanhagot*. 5½ x 8¼, 192 pp, Quality PB, ISBN 1-58023-186-1 **$16.95**

Our Dance with God: Finding Prayer, Perspective and Meaning in the Stories of Our Lives *By Karyn D. Kedar*
Inspiring spiritual insight to guide you on your life journeys and teach you to live and thrive in two conflicting worlds: the rational/material and the spiritual.
6 x 9, 176 pp, Quality PB, ISBN 1-58023-202-7 **$16.99**

Also Available: **The Dance of the Dolphin** (Hardcover edition of *Our Dance with God*)
6 x 9, 176 pp, Hardcover, ISBN 1-58023-154-3 **$19.95**

The Empty Chair: Finding Hope and Joy—Timeless Wisdom from a Hasidic Master, Rebbe Nachman of Breslov *Adapted by Moshe Mykoff and the Breslov Research Institute*
4 x 6, 128 pp, 2-color text, Deluxe PB w/flaps, ISBN 1-879045-67-2 **$9.95**

The Gentle Weapon: Prayers for Everyday and Not-So-Everyday Moments—
Timeless Wisdom from the Teachings of the Hasidic Master, Rebbe Nachman of Breslov
Adapted by Moshe Mykoff and S. C. Mizrahi, together with the Breslov Research Institute
4 x 6, 144 pp, 2-color text, Deluxe PB w/flaps, ISBN 1-58023-022-9 **$9.95**

God Whispers: Stories of the Soul, Lessons of the Heart *By Karyn D. Kedar*
6 x 9, 176 pp, Quality PB, ISBN 1-58023-088-1 **$15.95**

An Orphan in History: One Man's Triumphant Search for His Jewish Roots
By Paul Cowan. Afterword by Rachel Cowan. 6 x 9, 288 pp, Quality PB, ISBN 1-58023-135-7 **$16.95**

Restful Reflections: Nighttime Inspiration to Calm the Soul, Based on Jewish Wisdom
By Rabbi Kerry M. Olitzky & Rabbi Lori Forman 4½ x 6½, 448 pp, Quality PB, ISBN 1-58023-091-1 **$15.95**

Sacred Intentions: Daily Inspiration to Strengthen the Spirit, Based on Jewish Wisdom
By Rabbi Kerry M. Olitzky and Rabbi Lori Forman 4½ x 6½, 448 pp, Quality PB, ISBN 1-58023-061-X **$15.95**

Kabbalah/Mysticism/Enneagram

Seek My Face: A Jewish Mystical Theology
By Dr. Arthur Green
This classic work of contemporary Jewish theology, revised and updated, is a profound, deeply personal statement of the lasting truths of Jewish mysticism and the basic faith claims of Judaism. A tool for anyone seeking the elusive presence of God in the world. 6 x 9, 304 pp, Quality PB, ISBN 1-58023-130-6 **$19.95**

Zohar: Annotated & Explained
Translation and annotation by Dr. Daniel C. Matt. Foreword by Andrew Harvey
Offers insightful yet unobtrusive commentary to the masterpiece of Jewish mysticism that explains references and mystical symbols, shares wisdom of spiritual masters, and clarifies the *Zohar*'s bold claim: We have always been taught that we need God, but in order to manifest in the world, God needs us.
5½ x 8¼, 160 pp, Quality PB, ISBN 1-893361-51-9 **$15.99** *(A SkyLight Paths book)*

Cast in God's Image: Discover Your Personality Type Using the Enneagram and Kabbalah
By Rabbi Howard A. Addison
7 x 9, 176 pp, Quality PB, Layflat binding, 20+ journaling exercises, ISBN 1-58023-124-1 **$16.95**

Ehyeh: A Kabbalah for Tomorrow *By Dr. Arthur Green*
6 x 9, 224 pp, Quality PB, ISBN 1-58023-213-2 **$16.99**; Hardcover, ISBN 1-58023-125-X **$21.99**

The Enneagram and Kabbalah: Reading Your Soul *By Rabbi Howard A. Addison*
6 x 9, 176 pp, Quality PB, ISBN 1-58023-001-6 **$15.95**

Finding Joy: A Practical Spiritual Guide to Happiness *By Dannel I. Schwartz with Mark Hass*
6 x 9, 192 pp, Quality PB, ISBN 1-58023-009-1 **$14.95**; Hardcover, ISBN 1-879045-53-2 **$19.95**

The Gift of Kabbalah: Discovering the Secrets of Heaven, Renewing Your Life on Earth
By Tamar Frankiel, Ph.D.
6 x 9, 256 pp, Quality PB, ISBN 1-58023-141-1 **$16.95**; Hardcover, ISBN 1-58023-108-X **$21.95**

The Way Into Jewish Mystical Tradition *By Lawrence Kushner*
6 x 9, 224 pp, Quality PB, ISBN 1-58023-200-0 **$18.99**; Hardcover, ISBN 1-58023-029-6 **$21.95**

Life Cycle
Marriage / Parenting / Family / Aging

Jewish Fathers: A Legacy of Love
Photographs by Lloyd Wolf. Essays by Paula Wolfson. Foreword by Harold S. Kushner.
Honors the role of contemporary Jewish fathers in America. Each father tells in his own words what it means to be a parent and Jewish, and what he learned from his own father. Insightful photos. 9½ x 9⅞, 144 pp with 100+ duotone photos, Hardcover, ISBN 1-58023-204-3 **$30.00**

The New Jewish Baby Album: Creating and Celebrating the Beginning of a Spiritual Life—A Jewish Lights Companion
By the Editors at Jewish Lights. Foreword by Anita Diamant. Preface by Sandy Eisenberg Sasso.
A spiritual keepsake that will be treasured for generations. More than just a memory book, *shows you how—and why it's important*—to create a Jewish home and a Jewish life. 8 x 10, 64 pp, Deluxe Padded Hardcover, Full-color illus., ISBN 1-58023-138-1 **$19.95**

The Jewish Pregnancy Book: A Resource for the Soul, Body & Mind during Pregnancy, Birth & the First Three Months
By Sandy Falk, M.D., and Rabbi Daniel Judson, with Steven A. Rapp
Includes medical information on fetal development, pre-natal testing and more, from a liberal Jewish perspective; prenatal *Aleph-Bet* yoga; and prayers and rituals for each stage of pregnancy. 7 x 10, 208 pp, Quality PB, b/w illus., ISBN 1-58023-178-0 **$16.95**

Celebrating Your New Jewish Daughter: Creating Jewish Ways to Welcome Baby Girls into the Covenant—New and Traditional Ceremonies
By Debra Nussbaum Cohen 6 x 9, 272 pp, Quality PB, ISBN 1-58023-090-3 **$18.95**

The New Jewish Baby Book: Names, Ceremonies & Customs—A Guide for Today's Families *By Anita Diamant* 6 x 9, 336 pp, Quality PB, ISBN 1-879045-28-1 **$18.95**

Parenting As a Spiritual Journey: Deepening Ordinary and Extraordinary Events into Sacred Occasions *By Rabbi Nancy Fuchs-Kreimer* 6 x 9, 224 pp, Quality PB, ISBN 1-58023-016-4 **$16.95**

Embracing the Covenant: Converts to Judaism Talk About Why & How
Edited and with introductions by Rabbi Allan Berkowitz and Patti Moskovitz
6 x 9, 192 pp, Quality PB, ISBN 1-879045-50-8 **$16.95**

The Guide to Jewish Interfaith Family Life: An InterfaithFamily.com Handbook
Edited by Ronnie Friedland and Edmund Case 6 x 9, 384 pp, Quality PB, ISBN 1-58023-153-5 **$18.95**

Introducing My Faith and My Community
The Jewish Outreach Institute Guide for the Christian in a Jewish Interfaith Relationship
By Rabbi Kerry M. Olitzky 6 x 9, 176 pp, Quality PB, ISBN 1-58023-192-6 **$16.99**

Making a Successful Jewish Interfaith Marriage: The Jewish Outreach Institute Guide to Opportunities, Challenges and Resources
By Rabbi Kerry M. Olitzky with Joan Peterson Littman 6 x 9, 176 pp, Quality PB, ISBN 1-58023-170-5 **$16.95**

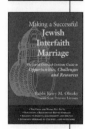

How to Be a Perfect Stranger, 3rd Edition: The Essential Religious Etiquette Handbook *Edited by Stuart M. Matlins and Arthur J. Magida*
The indispensable guide to the rituals and celebrations of the major religions and denominations in North America from the perspective of an interested guest of any other faith. 6 x 9, 432 pp, Quality PB, ISBN 1-893361-67-5 **$19.95** *(A SkyLight Paths book)*

The Creative Jewish Wedding Book: A Hands-On Guide to New & Old Traditions, Ceremonies & Celebrations *By Gabrielle Kaplan-Mayer*
Provides the tools to create the most meaningful Jewish traditional or alternative wedding by using ritual elements to express your unique style and spirituality.
9 x 9, 288 pp, b/w photos, Quality PB, ISBN 1-58023-194-2 **$19.99**

Divorce Is a Mitzvah: A Practical Guide to Finding Wholeness and Holiness When Your Marriage Dies *By Rabbi Perry Netter. Afterword by Rabbi Laura Geller.*
6 x 9, 224 pp, Quality PB, ISBN 1-58023-172-1 **$16.95**

A Heart of Wisdom: Making the Jewish Journey from Midlife through the Elder Years
Edited by Susan Berrin. Foreword by Harold Kushner. 6 x 9, 384 pp, Quality PB, ISBN 1-58023-051-2 **$18.95**

So That Your Values Live On: Ethical Wills and How to Prepare Them
Edited by Jack Riemer and Nathaniel Stampfer 6 x 9, 272 pp, Quality PB, ISBN 1-879045-34-6 **$18.95**

Meditation

The Handbook of Jewish Meditation Practices
A Guide for Enriching the Sabbath and Other Days of Your Life
By Rabbi David A. Cooper
Easy-to-learn meditation techniques for use on the Sabbath and every day, to help us return to the roots of traditional Jewish spirituality where Shabbat is a state of mind and soul. 6 x 9, 208 pp, Quality PB, ISBN 1-58023-102-0 **$16.95**

Discovering Jewish Meditation: Instruction & Guidance for Learning an Ancient
Spiritual Practice By Nan Fink Gefen, Ph.D. 6 x 9, 208 pp, Quality PB, ISBN 1-58023-067-9 **$16.95**

A Heart of Stillness: A Complete Guide to Learning the Art of Meditation
By Rabbi David A. Cooper 5½ x 8½, 272 pp, Quality PB, ISBN 1-893361-03-9 **$16.95**
(A SkyLight Paths book)

Meditation from the Heart of Judaism: Today's Teachers Share Their
Practices, Techniques, and Faith Edited by Avram Davis
6 x 9, 256 pp, Quality PB, ISBN 1-58023-049-0 **$16.95**

Silence, Simplicity & Solitude: A Complete Guide to Spiritual Retreat at Home
By Rabbi David A. Cooper 5½ x 8½, 336 pp, Quality PB, ISBN 1-893361-04-7 **$16.95**
(A SkyLight Paths book)

Three Gates to Meditation Practice: A Personal Journey into Sufism,
Buddhism, and Judaism By Rabbi David A. Cooper
5½ x 8½, 240 pp, Quality PB, ISBN 1-893361-22-5 **$16.95** (A SkyLight Paths book)

The Way of Flame: A Guide to the Forgotten Mystical Tradition of Jewish Meditation
By Avram Davis 4½ x 8, 176 pp, Quality PB, ISBN 1-58023-060-1 **$15.95**

Ritual/Sacred Practice/Journaling

The Jewish Dream Book: The Key to Opening the Inner Meaning of
Your Dreams By Vanessa L. Ochs with Elizabeth Ochs; Full-color illus. by Kristina Swarner
Instructions for how modern people can perform ancient Jewish dream practices and dream interpretations drawn from the Jewish wisdom tradition. For anyone who wants to understand their dreams—and themselves.
8 x 8, 120 pp, Full-color illus., Deluxe PB w/flaps, ISBN 1-58023-132-2 **$16.95**

The Jewish Journaling Book: How to Use Jewish Tradition to Write
Your Life & Explore Your Soul By Janet Ruth Falon
Details the history of Jewish journaling throughout biblical and modern times, and teaches specific journaling techniques to help you create and maintain a vital journal, from a Jewish perspective. 8 x 8, 304 pp, Deluxe PB w/flaps, ISBN 1-58023-203-5 **$18.99**

The Rituals & Practices of a Jewish Life: A Handbook for Personal Spiritual
Renewal Edited by Rabbi Kerry M. Olitzky and Rabbi Daniel Judson
6 x 9, 272 pp, illus., Quality PB, ISBN 1-58023-169-1 **$18.95**

The Book of Jewish Sacred Practices: CLAL's Guide to Everyday & Holiday
Rituals & Blessings Edited by Rabbi Irwin Kula and Vanessa L. Ochs, Ph.D.
6 x 9, 368 pp, Quality PB, ISBN 1-58023-152-7 **$18.95**

Science Fiction/
Mystery & Detective Fiction

Mystery Midrash: An Anthology of Jewish Mystery & Detective Fiction
Edited by Lawrence W. Raphael. Preface by Joel Siegel.
6 x 9, 304 pp, Quality PB, ISBN 1-58023-055-5 **$16.95**

Criminal Kabbalah: An Intriguing Anthology of Jewish Mystery & Detective Fiction
Edited by Lawrence W. Raphael. Foreword by Laurie R. King.
6 x 9, 256 pp, Quality PB, ISBN 1-58023-109-8 **$16.95**

More Wandering Stars: An Anthology of Outstanding Stories of Jewish Fantasy and
Science Fiction Edited by Jack Dann. Introduction by Isaac Asimov.
6 x 9, 192 pp, Quality PB, ISBN 1-58023-063-6 **$16.95**

Wandering Stars: An Anthology of Jewish Fantasy & Science Fiction
Edited by Jack Dann. Introduction by Isaac Asimov.
6 x 9, 272 pp, Quality PB, ISBN 1-58023-005-9 **$16.95**

Spirituality

The Alphabet of Paradise: An A–Z of Spirituality for Everyday Life
By Rabbi Howard Cooper
In twenty-six engaging chapters, Cooper spiritually illuminates the subjects of our daily lives—A to Z—examining these sources by using an ancient Jewish mystical method of interpretation that reveals both the literal and more allusive meanings of each. 5 x 7¼, 224 pp, Quality PB, ISBN 1-893361-80-2 **$16.95** *(A SkyLight Paths book)*

Does the Soul Survive?: A Jewish Journey to Belief in Afterlife, Past Lives & Living with Purpose *By Rabbi Elie Kaplan Spitz. Foreword by Brian L. Weiss, M.D.*
Spitz relates his own experiences and those shared with him by people he has worked with as a rabbi, and shows us that belief in afterlife and past lives, so often approached with reluctance, is in fact true to Jewish tradition.
6 x 9, 288 pp, Quality PB, ISBN 1-58023-165-9 **$16.99**; Hardcover, ISBN 1-58023-094-6 **$21.95**

First Steps to a New Jewish Spirit: Reb Zalman's Guide to Recapturing the Intimacy & Ecstasy in Your Relationship with God
By Rabbi Zalman M. Schachter-Shalomi with Donald Gropman
An extraordinary spiritual handbook that restores psychic and physical vigor by introducing us to new models and alternative ways of practicing Judaism. Offers meditation and contemplation exercises for enriching the most important aspects of everyday life. 6 x 9, 144 pp, Quality PB, ISBN 1-58023-182-9 **$16.95**

God in Our Relationships: Spirituality between People from the Teachings of Martin Buber *By Rabbi Dennis S. Ross*
On the eightieth anniversary of Buber's classic work, we can discover new answers to critical issues in our lives. Inspiring examples from Ross's own life—as congregational rabbi, father, hospital chaplain, social worker, and husband—illustrate Buber's difficult-to-understand ideas about how we encounter God and each other. 5½ x 8½, 160 pp, Quality PB, ISBN 1-58023-147-0 **$16.95**

The Jewish Lights Spirituality Handbook: A Guide to Understanding, Exploring & Living a Spiritual Life *Edited by Stuart M. Matlins*
What exactly is "Jewish" about spirituality? How do I make it a part of my life? Fifty of today's foremost spiritual leaders share their ideas and experience with us.
6 x 9, 456 pp, Quality PB, ISBN 1-58023-093-8 **$19.99**; Hardcover, ISBN 1-58023-100-4 **$24.95**

Bringing the Psalms to Life: How to Understand and Use the Book of Psalms
By Dr. Daniel F. Polish
6 x 9, 208 pp, Quality PB, ISBN 1-58023-157-8 **$16.95**; Hardcover, ISBN 1-58023-077-6 **$21.95**

God & the Big Bang: Discovering Harmony between Science & Spirituality
By Dr. Daniel C. Matt 6 x 9, 216 pp, Quality PB, ISBN 1-879045-89-3 **$16.95**

Godwrestling—Round 2: Ancient Wisdom, Future Paths
By Rabbi Arthur Waskow 6 x 9, 352 pp, Quality PB, ISBN 1-879045-72-9 **$18.95**

One God Clapping: The Spiritual Path of a Zen Rabbi *By Rabbi Alan Lew with Sherril Jaffe*
5½ x 8½, 336 pp, Quality PB, ISBN 1-58023-115-2 **$16.95**

The Path of Blessing: Experiencing the Energy and Abundance of the Divine
By Rabbi Marcia Prager 5½ x 8½, 240 pp, Quality PB, ISBN 1-58023-148-9 **$16.95**

Six Jewish Spiritual Paths: A Rationalist Looks at Spirituality *By Rabbi Rifat Sonsino*
6 x 9, 208 pp, Quality PB, ISBN 1-58023-167-5 **$16.95**; Hardcover, ISBN 1-58023-095-4 **$21.95**

Soul Judaism: Dancing with God into a New Era
By Rabbi Wayne Dosick 5½ x 8½, 304 pp, Quality PB, ISBN 1-58023-053-9 **$16.95**

Stepping Stones to Jewish Spiritual Living: Walking the Path Morning, Noon, and Night *By Rabbi James L. Mirel and Karen Bonnell Werth*
6 x 9, 240 pp, Quality PB, ISBN 1-58023-074-1 **$16.95**; Hardcover, ISBN 1-58023-003-2 **$21.95**

There Is No Messiah... and You're It: The Stunning Transformation of Judaism's Most Provocative Idea *By Rabbi Robert N. Levine, D.D.*
6 x 9, 192 pp, Hardcover, ISBN 1-58023-173-X **$21.95**

These Are the Words: A Vocabulary of Jewish Spiritual Life *By Dr. Arthur Green*
6 x 9, 304 pp, Quality PB, ISBN 1-58023-107-1 **$18.95**

Spirituality/Lawrence Kushner

The Book of Letters: A Mystical Hebrew Alphabet
Popular Hardcover Edition, 6 x 9, 80 pp, 2-color text, ISBN 1-879045-00-1 **$24.95**
Deluxe Gift Edition with slipcase, 9 x 12, 80 pp, 4-color text, Hardcover, ISBN 1-879045-01-X **$79.95**
Collector's Limited Edition, 9 x 12, 80 pp, gold foil embossed pages, w/limited edition silkscreened print, ISBN 1-879045-04-4 **$349.00**

The Book of Miracles: A Young Person's Guide to Jewish Spiritual Awareness
All-new illustrations by the author
6 x 9, 96 pp, 2-color illus., Hardcover, ISBN 1-879045-78-8 **$16.95** *For ages 9–13*

The Book of Words: Talking Spiritual Life, Living Spiritual Talk
6 x 9, 160 pp, Quality PB, ISBN 1-58023-020-2 **$16.95**

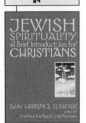

Eyes Remade for Wonder: A Lawrence Kushner Reader
Introduction by Thomas Moore
6 x 9, 240 pp, Quality PB, ISBN 1-58023-042-3 **$18.95;** Hardcover, ISBN 1-58023-014-8 **$23.95**

God Was in This Place & I, i Did Not Know
Finding Self, Spirituality and Ultimate Meaning
6 x 9, 192 pp, Quality PB, ISBN 1-879045-33-8 **$16.95**

Honey from the Rock: An Introduction to Jewish Mysticism
6 x 9, 176 pp, Quality PB, ISBN 1-58023-073-3 **$16.95**

Invisible Lines of Connection: Sacred Stories of the Ordinary
5½ x 8½, 160 pp, Quality PB, ISBN 1-879045-98-2 **$15.95**

Jewish Spirituality—A Brief Introduction for Christians
5½ x 8½, 112 pp, Quality PB Original, ISBN 1-58023-150-0 **$12.95**

The River of Light: Jewish Mystical Awareness
6 x 9, 192 pp, Quality PB, ISBN 1-58023-096-2 **$16.95**

The Way Into Jewish Mystical Tradition
6 x 9, 224 pp, Quality PB, ISBN 1-58023-200-0 **$18.99;** Hardcover, ISBN 1-58023-029-6 **$21.95**

Spirituality/Prayer

Pray Tell: A Hadassah Guide to Jewish Prayer
By Rabbi Jules Harlow, with contributions from Tamara Cohen, Rochelle Furstenberg, Rabbi Daniel Gordis, Leora Tanenbaum, and many others
A guide to traditional Jewish prayer enriched with insight and wisdom from a broad variety of viewpoints—from Orthodox, Conservative, Reform, and Reconstructionist Judaism to New Age and feminist.
8½ x 11, 400 pp, Quality PB, ISBN 1-58023-163-2 **$29.95**

My People's Prayer Book Series
Traditional Prayers, Modern Commentaries
Edited by Rabbi Lawrence A. Hoffman
Provides diverse and exciting commentary to the traditional liturgy, helping modern men and women find new wisdom in Jewish prayer, and bring liturgy into their lives.

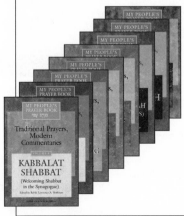

Each book includes Hebrew text, modern translation, and commentaries from all perspectives of the Jewish world.

Vol. 1—The *Sh'ma* and Its Blessings
7 x 10, 168 pp, Hardcover, ISBN 1-879045-79-6 **$23.95**

Vol. 2—The *Amidah*
7 x 10, 240 pp, Hardcover, ISBN 1-879045-80-X **$24.95**

Vol. 3—*P'sukei D'zimrah* (Morning Psalms)
7 x 10, 240 pp, Hardcover, ISBN 1-879045-81-8 **$24.95**

Vol. 4—*Seder K'riat Hatorah* (The Torah Service)
7 x 10, 264 pp, Hardcover, ISBN 1-879045-82-6 **$23.95**

Vol. 5—*Birkhot Hashachar* (Morning Blessings)
7 x 10, 240 pp, Hardcover, ISBN 1-879045-83-4 **$24.95**

Vol. 6—*Tachanun* and Concluding Prayers
7 x 10, 240 pp, Hardcover, ISBN 1-879045-84-2 **$24.95**

Vol. 7—Shabbat at Home
7 x 10, 240 pp, Hardcover, ISBN 1-879045-85-0 **$24.95**

Vol. 8—*Kabbalat Shabbat* (Welcoming Shabbat in the Synagogue)
7 x 10, 240 pp, Hardcover, ISBN 1-58023-121-7 **$24.99**

Spirituality/The Way Into... Series

The Way Into... Series offers an accessible and highly usable "guided tour" of the Jewish faith, people, history and beliefs—in total, an introduction to Judaism that will enable you to understand and interact with the sacred texts of the Jewish tradition. Each volume is written by a leading contemporary scholar and teacher, and explores one key aspect of Judaism. *The Way Into...* enables all readers to achieve a real sense of Jewish cultural literacy through guided study.

The Way Into Encountering God in Judaism *By Neil Gillman*
6 x 9, 240 pp, Quality PB, ISBN 1-58023-199-3 **$18.99**; Hardcover, ISBN 1-58023-025-3 **$21.95**

Also Available: **The Jewish Approach to God: A Brief Introduction for Christians**
By Neil Gillman 5½ x 8½, 192 pp, Quality PB, ISBN 1-58023-190-X **$16.95**

The Way Into Jewish Mystical Tradition *By Lawrence Kushner*
6 x 9, 224 pp, Quality PB, ISBN 1-58023-200-0 **$18.99**; Hardcover, ISBN 1-58023-029-6 **$21.95**

The Way Into Jewish Prayer *By Lawrence A. Hoffman*
6 x 9, 224 pp, Quality PB, ISBN 1-58023-201-9 **$18.99**; Hardcover, ISBN 1-58023-027-X **$21.95**

The Way Into Torah *By Norman J. Cohen*
6 x 9, 176 pp, Quality PB, ISBN 1-58023-198-5 **$16.99**; Hardcover, ISBN 1-58023-028-8 **$21.95**

Spirituality in the Workplace

Being God's Partner
How to Find the Hidden Link Between Spirituality and Your Work
By Rabbi Jeffrey K. Salkin. Introduction by Norman Lear.
6 x 9, 192 pp, Quality PB, ISBN 1-879045-65-6 **$17.95**

The Business Bible: 10 New Commandments for Bringing Spirituality & Ethical
Values into the Workplace *By Rabbi Wayne Dosick*
5½ x 8½, 208 pp, Quality PB, ISBN 1-58023-101-2 **$14.95**

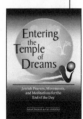

Spirituality and Wellness

Aleph-Bet Yoga
Embodying the Hebrew Letters for Physical and Spiritual Well-Being
By Steven A. Rapp. Foreword by Tamar Frankiel, Ph.D., and Judy Greenfeld. Preface by Hart Lazer
7 x 10, 128 pp, b/w photos, Quality PB, Layflat binding, ISBN 1-58023-162-4 **$16.95**

Entering the Temple of Dreams
Jewish Prayers, Movements, and Meditations for the End of the Day
By Tamar Frankiel, Ph.D., and Judy Greenfeld
7 x 10, 192 pp, illus., Quality PB, ISBN 1-58023-079-2 **$16.95**

Jewish Paths toward Healing and Wholeness: A Personal Guide to Dealing
with Suffering *By Rabbi Kerry M. Olitzky. Foreword by Debbie Friedman.*
6 x 9, 192 pp, Quality PB, ISBN 1-58023-068-7 **$15.95**

Minding the Temple of the Soul
Balancing Body, Mind, and Spirit through Traditional Jewish Prayer, Movement, and
Meditation *By Tamar Frankiel, Ph.D., and Judy Greenfeld*
7 x 10, 184 pp, illus., Quality PB, ISBN 1-879045-64-8 **$16.95**
Audiotape of the Blessings and Meditations: 60 min. **$9.95**
Videotape of the Movements and Meditations: 46 min. **$20.00**

Spirituality/Women's Interest

The Quotable Jewish Woman: Wisdom, Inspiration & Humor from the Mind & Heart *Edited and compiled by Elaine Bernstein Partnow*
The definitive collection of ideas, reflections, humor, and wit of over 300 Jewish women.
6 x 9, 496 pp, Hardcover, ISBN 1-58023-193-4 **$29.99**

Lifecycles, Vol. 1: Jewish Women on Life Passages & Personal Milestones
Edited and with introductions by Rabbi Debra Orenstein 6 x 9, 480 pp, Quality PB, ISBN 1-58023-018-0 **$19.95**

Lifecycles, Vol. 2: Jewish Women on Biblical Themes in Contemporary Life
Edited and with introductions by Rabbi Debra Orenstein and Rabbi Jane Rachel Litman
6 x 9, 464 pp, Quality PB, ISBN 1-58023-019-9 **$19.95**

Moonbeams: A Hadassah Rosh Hodesh Guide *Edited by Carol Diament, Ph.D.*
8½ x 11, 240 pp, Quality PB, ISBN 1-58023-099-7 **$20.00**

ReVisions: Seeing Torah through a Feminist Lens *By Rabbi Elyse Goldstein*
5½ x 8½, 224 pp, Quality PB, ISBN 1-58023-117-9 **$16.95**

White Fire: A Portrait of Women Spiritual Leaders in America
By Rabbi Malka Drucker. Photographs by Gay Block.
7 x 10, 320 pp, 30+ b/w photos, Hardcover, ISBN 1-893361-64-0 **$24.95** *(A SkyLight Paths book)*

Women of the Wall: Claiming Sacred Ground at Judaism's Holy Site
Edited by Phyllis Chesler and Rivka Haut 6 x 9, 496 pp, b/w photos, Hardcover, ISBN 1-58023-161-6 **$34.95**

The Women's Haftarah Commentary: New Insights from Women Rabbis on the 54 Weekly Haftarah Portions, the 5 Megillot & Special Shabbatot
Edited by Rabbi Elyse Goldstein 6 x 9, 560 pp, Hardcover, ISBN 1-58023-133-0 **$39.99**

The Women's Torah Commentary: New Insights from Women Rabbis on the 54 Weekly Torah Portions *Edited by Rabbi Elyse Goldstein*
6 x 9, 496 pp, Hardcover, ISBN 1-58023-076-8 **$34.95**

The Year Mom Got Religion: One Woman's Midlife Journey into Judaism
By Lee Meyerhoff Hendler 6 x 9, 208 pp, Quality PB, ISBN 1-58023-070-9 **$15.95**

See Holidays for *The Women's Passover Companion: Women's Reflections on the Festival of Freedom* and *The Women's Seder Sourcebook: Rituals & Readings for Use at the Passover Seder.*

Travel

Israel—A Spiritual Travel Guide: A Companion for the Modern Jewish Pilgrim
By Rabbi Lawrence A. Hoffman 4¾ x 10, 256 pp, Quality PB, illus., ISBN 1-879045-56-7 **$18.95**
Also Available: **The Israel Mission Leader's Guide** ISBN 1-58023-085-7 **$4.95**

12 Steps

100 Blessings Every Day
Daily Twelve Step Recovery Affirmations, Exercises for Personal Growth & Renewal Reflecting Seasons of the Jewish Year
By Rabbi Kerry M. Olitzky. Foreword by Rabbi Neil Gillman.
One-day-at-a-time monthly format. Reflects on the rhythm of the Jewish calendar to bring insight to recovery from addictions.
4½ x 6¼, 432 pp, Quality PB, ISBN 1-879045-30-3 **$15.99**

Recovery from Codependence: A Jewish Twelve Steps Guide to Healing Your Soul
By Rabbi Kerry M. Olitzky 6 x 9, 160 pp, Quality PB, ISBN 1-879045-32-X **$13.95**

Renewed Each Day: Daily Twelve Step Recovery Meditations Based on the Bible
By Rabbi Kerry M. Olitzky and Aaron Z.
Vol. 1—Genesis & Exodus: 6 x 9, 224 pp, Quality PB, ISBN 1-879045-12-5 **$14.95**
Vol. 2—Leviticus, Numbers & Deuteronomy: 6 x 9, 280 pp, Quality PB, ISBN 1-879045-13-3 **$14.95**

Twelve Jewish Steps to Recovery: A Personal Guide to Turning from Alcoholism & Other Addictions—Drugs, Food, Gambling, Sex...
By Rabbi Kerry M. Olitzky and Stuart A. Copans, M.D. Preface by Abraham J. Twerski, M.D.
6 x 9, 144 pp, Quality PB, ISBN 1-879045-09-5 **$14.95**

Theology/Philosophy

Aspects of Rabbinic Theology
By Solomon Schechter. New Introduction by Dr. Neil Gillman.
6 x 9, 448 pp, Quality PB, ISBN 1-879045-24-9 **$19.95**

Broken Tablets: Restoring the Ten Commandments and Ourselves
Edited by Rachel S. Mikva. Introduction by Lawrence Kushner. Afterword by Arnold Jacob Wolf.
6 x 9, 192 pp, Quality PB, ISBN 1-58023-158-6 **$16.95**; Hardcover, ISBN 1-58023-066-0 **$21.95**

Creating an Ethical Jewish Life
A Practical Introduction to Classic Teachings on How to Be a Jew
By Dr. Byron L. Sherwin and Seymour J. Cohen
6 x 9, 336 pp, Quality PB, ISBN 1-58023-114-4 **$19.95**

The Death of Death: Resurrection and Immortality in Jewish Thought
By Dr. Neil Gillman 6 x 9, 336 pp, Quality PB, ISBN 1-58023-081-4 **$18.95**

Evolving Halakhah: A Progressive Approach to Traditional Jewish Law
By Rabbi Dr. Moshe Zemer
6 x 9, 480 pp, Quality PB, ISBN 1-58023-127-6 **$29.95**; Hardcover, ISBN 1-58023-002-4 **$40.00**

Hasidic Tales: Annotated & Explained
By Rabbi Rami Shapiro. Foreword by Andrew Harvey, SkyLight Illuminations series editor.
5½ x 8½, 240 pp, Quality PB, ISBN 1-893361-86-1 **$16.95** *(A SkyLight Paths Book)*

A Heart of Many Rooms: Celebrating the Many Voices within Judaism
By Dr. David Hartman 6 x 9, 352 pp, Quality PB, ISBN 1-58023-156-X **$19.95**

The Hebrew Prophets: Selections Annotated & Explained
Translation & Annotation by Rabbi Rami Shapiro. Foreword by Zalman M. Schachter-Shalomi
5½ x 8½, 224 pp, Quality PB, ISBN 1-59473-037-7 **$16.99** *(A SkyLight Paths book)*

Keeping Faith with the Psalms: Deepen Your Relationship with God Using the
Book of Psalms *By Daniel F. Polish* 6 x 9, 272 pp, Hardcover, ISBN 1-58023-179-9 **$24.95**

The Last Trial
On the Legends and Lore of the Command to Abraham to Offer Isaac as a Sacrifice
By Shalom Spiegel. New Introduction by Judah Goldin.
6 x 9, 208 pp, Quality PB, ISBN 1-879045-29-X **$18.95**

A Living Covenant: The Innovative Spirit in Traditional Judaism
By Dr. David Hartman 6 x 9, 368 pp, Quality PB, ISBN 1-58023-011-3 **$18.95**

Love and Terror in the God Encounter
The Theological Legacy of Rabbi Joseph B. Soloveitchik
By Dr. David Hartman
6 x 9, 240 pp, Quality PB, ISBN 1-58023-176-4 **$19.95**; Hardcover, ISBN 1-58023-112-8 **$25.00**

Seeking the Path to Life
Theological Meditations on God and the Nature of People, Love, Life and Death
By Rabbi Ira F. Stone 6 x 9, 160 pp, Quality PB, ISBN 1-879045-47-8 **$14.95**

The Spirit of Renewal: Finding Faith after the Holocaust
By Rabbi Edward Feld 6 x 9, 224 pp, Quality PB, ISBN 1-879045-40-0 **$16.95**

Tormented Master: *The Life and Spiritual Quest of Rabbi Nahman of Bratslav*
By Dr. Arthur Green 6 x 9, 416 pp, Quality PB, ISBN 1-879045-11-7 **$19.99**

Your Word Is Fire: The Hasidic Masters on Contemplative Prayer
Edited and translated by Dr. Arthur Green and Barry W. Holtz
6 x 9, 160 pp, Quality PB, ISBN 1-879045-25-7 **$15.95**

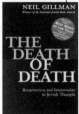
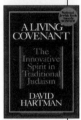

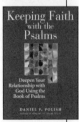

I Am Jewish
Personal Reflections Inspired by the Last Words of Daniel Pearl

Almost 150 Jews—both famous and not—from all walks of life, from all around the world, write about Identity, Heritage, Covenant / Chosenness and Faith, Humanity and Ethnicity, and *Tikkun Olam* and Justice.

Edited by Judea and Ruth Pearl
6 x 9, 304 pp, Hardcover, ISBN 1-58023-183-7 **$24.99**

Download a free copy of the *I Am Jewish Teacher's Guide* at our website:
www.jewishlights.com

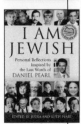

About Jewish Lights

People of all faiths and backgrounds yearn for books that attract, engage, educate, and spiritually inspire.

Our principal goal is to stimulate thought and help all people learn about who the Jewish People are, where they come from, and what the future can be made to hold. While people of our diverse Jewish heritage are the primary audience, our books speak to people in the Christian world as well and will broaden their understanding of Judaism and the roots of their own faith.

We bring to you authors who are at the forefront of spiritual thought and experience. While each has something different to say, they all say it in a voice that you can hear.

Our books are designed to welcome you and then to engage, stimulate, and inspire. We judge our success not only by whether or not our books are beautiful and commercially successful, but by whether or not they make a difference in your life.

For your information and convenience, at the back of this book we have provided a list of other Jewish Lights books you might find interesting and useful. They cover all the categories of your life:

Stuart M. Matlins, Publisher

Or phone, fax, mail or e-mail to: **JEWISH LIGHTS Publishing**
Sunset Farm Offices, Route 4 • P.O. Box 237 • Woodstock, Vermont 05091
Tel: (802) 457-4000 • Fax: (802) 457-4004 • www.jewishlights.com
Credit card orders: (800) 962-4544 (8:30AM–5:30PM ET Monday–Friday)
Generous discounts on quantity orders. SATISFACTION GUARANTEED. Prices subject to change.